FROM CRACK TO CHRIST

FROM CRACK TO CHRIST

TWENTY YEARS LATER

DR. STEPHEN B. TOWNS, SR.

FERVENT ASCENT MEDIA
BOOKS
Impact lives, then worlds.

Every transformation story needs a remarkable protagonist who personifies the power of God in the work of salvation. Stephen is that. As bad as Stephen's story made his life look in this world, this masterful account of his redemption sure makes God look good.

Rev. M.D. "Doc" Bass
Saint Louis, MO

It was hard to contain the jubilant exuberance I felt upon hearing *From Crack to Christ* penned by Dr. Stephen B. Towns would be re-released. The book was written with much candor and transparency, and those reading it will be immensely blessed!

Dr. Z. Michelle Hughes
Empowered to Change LLC

I am ever so grateful to know Dr. Stephen Towns. In our time working together, he imparted so much wisdom upon me. To this day his advice still rings true. *From Crack to Christ* is an amazing testimony of God's love, grace, and power!

Darryl Thompson
Chesterfield, VA

God set the stage, but you raised the curtains and masterfully penned the miraculous transformation of your life. You took us on a journey and you've left us believing that there is absolutely nothing too hard for God. Thank you for your bold, vivid, authentic testimony. Because of that, *From Crack to Christ* breeds healing and hope in this real life. In that, Dr. Towns, God is well-pleased!

Lady Kimberly Towns
Real Life Ministries, Church of God in Christ

Dr. Stephen B. Towns, Sr. has written a very compelling work that, in ways, many can find a portion, if not all, of themselves in his past experience of living a life without Christ. Any church in the 21st century that has an outreach ministry, and or a counseling department, and deals exclusively with substance abuse and addiction will find *From Crack to Christ: 20 Years Later* beneficial as a valuable resource. This book connects both practical, mental, and spiritual realities of drug addiction and deliverance therefrom, which is why this book is being recommended to clergy, laity, and professional addiction counselors.

Min. Trevor T. Delaney, M.Div.
Real Life Ministries – Youth Minister

Dr. Towns, I believe your courage and testimony is truly orchestrated by God. Your transparency about making mistakes, having struggles in life, and not allowing them to define you is truly powerful. Continue to share the God in you! You are a blessing!

Louis Young
Hopefinders, Inc.

At the construction of this vivid autobiography, I was in my late teens, so full comprehension for me didn't come until I grew as a man. As an author myself, the details in my dad's story gravitated me toward wanting to read more and more! It's that ability he possesses that lets me know God put the right message in the best man. Keep shining, Pops!

Gallo
Music Artist

This writing reveals the reluctant limitation of humanity in contrast to the unlimited power of God's divinity. Our hearts embrace the transparency of this book which reminds us God's power is yet transformational. What a template and absolute road map to those who struggle with the perpetual pain of this fight. This is indeed a must-have for every support group and ministry-oriented church looking to meet the needs of the distressed.

Supt. Michael B. Golden, Jr.
Pastor of Greater Emmanuel Temple, Hampton VA
Chairman of the COGIC International Men's Department

Life's vicissitudes are seemingly recrementitious in proportion to the feeble vessels that carry them. Dr. Towns' bravery, ultimately, to negotiate through those horrid meanderings of addiction not only deserve commendation but serious reflection for anyone seeking levitation from abysmal ruin to compassion and refuge in Jesus Christ.

Bishop Chadwick F. Carlton
Jurisdictional Prelate – Republic of Korea, Church of God in Christ
Pastor, Temple of Healing Waters, Sterling, VA

The Stephen Towns story is an awesome testament of the transformational power of the Holy Spirit in an individual's life. People with deviant behavior struggling to overcome can find hope for deliverance from this story. Individuals married to spouses with addictions and behavioral problems, and praying parents dealing with troublesome children can receive encouragement from this story that affirms God is able to perform the impossible.

Today, Stephen is a responsible asset to his community in Richmond, Virginia and humanity. He has matriculated from a bachelors and masters program, to completing a doctoral program. He has a management position in the healthcare industry and is the Director of Health and Human Services of Grace 5 Jurisdiction, Virginia Church of God in Christ (COGIC), and is a consultant for the National Pastors and Elders Council's COGIC Health Commission. Called to the ministry in 1996, Stephen is now Pastor of Real Life Ministries COGIC and District Superintendent of Roanoke District COGIC, VA. Dr. Stephen Towns is a major asset of the evangelism and mission thrust of our jurisdictional ministry and I believe his ministry will bless your life.

Bishop Dwight L. Green, Sr.,
Prelate Grace 5 Jurisdiction Virginia Church of God in Christ, Inc.

ISBN: 978-1-9992283-8-5
www.ferventascent.com

Contents

DEDICATION

From Crack to Christ: Twenty Years Later is dedicated to:

My Grandmother, **Mother Odell Towns**, the Matriarch. Thank you for your unending prayers while the entire family was lost in sin. This book is still for you.

My brother, **Minister Marvin "Coach B." Bridges**. Thank you for your friendship, your support, your prayers, and your brotherly love. Thank you for being "the light that shines on a hill." This book is for you.

My first Richmond friend, **Minister Leon Person**. Thank you for over 40 years of fearless friendship. When I ran the point, I always knew exactly where you'd be on the wing! Recently, you also partnered with me in ministry, and we had such grand hopes for the future. This book is for you.

My friend, **Wilbur Papa Thomas**. You are not forgotten. This book remains for you.

FOREWORD

The transformation of Dr. Stephen Towns has been a miracle. The testimony of what God has done in his life has been incredible. I have been knowing him for nearly twenty years and seeing is believing. This man of God is the real deal! He had a reputation of being a man who used to roam the streets looking for trouble decades ago, but now he is a man of faith roaming the streets to minister to others.

If you are looking for hope, the first step is to look for it in the right places. Dr. Town's book, *From Crack to Christ: Twenty Years Later*, not only shows you that hope is available; he shares how to overcome in life. He takes the reader on a journey on how to transition from hopelessness to victory. This book is not only inspirational, but it is also transformational.

Stephen Towns masterfully touches the reader's heart through his transparency in this book. He willingly opens up about the challenges of addiction and how we can overcome through our relationship with Jesus Christ. That with just one encounter with Jesus, everything can change. Dr. Towns walks us through the process of falling into the arms of Jesus, trusting in God's character, and experiencing a life-changing encounter for all to witness.

This book is not only a testimony of what God has done in his life, but how God has touched so many other lives through it. I have personally witnessed how he has been promoted, elevated, and appointed to make a difference for a time such as this. His desire to help others get delivered and set free from the scourge of addiction is a joy to see. I enthusiastically recommend *From Crack to Christ: Twenty Years Later* to anyone who wants to help others in the midst of the struggle.

In His Service,
Wade S. Runge, DMin
Senior Pastor M3 Church
Chesterfield, Virginia

PREFACE

King Solomon penned in Ecclesiastes:

> [1] To every thing there is a season, and a time to every purpose under the heaven: [2] A time to be born, and a time to die; a time to plant, and a time to pluck up that which is planted; [3] A time to kill, and a time to heal; a time to break down, and a time to build up.

> —Ecclesiastes 3:1-3 (KJV)

This pericope of Scripture uncannily reflects my time thus far on God's green earth: from the beginning, with my first twenty-two years of experience growing of age in New Jersey; then, the next eighteen years overcoming a myriad of mature addictions in Virginia; and, finally, finding salvation at the age of forty. Now, at sixty-four years of age, I thank God that I don't look like what I've been through.

Honestly, what I've been through feels like three very distinct lifetimes. *From Crack to Christ: Twenty Years Later* chronicles a portion of my journey—arguably the darkest season of my life—then transitions to my encounter with a man named Jesus. Miracles, signs, and wonders jump off the pages as the gift of salvation, the results of fervent prayer, and God's unmerited favor are all blended and on display.

The year 2020 will forever be known as the year of the Covid-19 Pandemic and the year of people's unrest against racism. For me, I will recall this year as the year that God hit the "reset button". In many ways, it as if God is giving mankind a do-over. A do-over to end racism. A do-over to evaluate and redefine how we do church, and a do-over of how we care for each other, especially those less fortunate.

This "reset" move of God confirms that I need to do my part in fighting for those who are unable to fight for themselves. That includes the addicted. Being bi-vocational and also working in the healthcare industry, I understand the physical and behavioral health ramifications of addiction. On the other hand, I'm unsure if the healthcare industry understands and fully accepts the spiritual ability to overcome the condition of addiction.

I have been drug-, alcohol-, and tobacco-free since July of 1996 without a single event of indulgence. Not one. I have not taken a drag from a cigarette, sipped an ice-cold beer, or inhaled a hit of marijuana since July of 1996. It's not that I can't, but I choose not to. I have taken the power back over my temple, and it feels terrific!

I want others to experience freedom from the shackles of bondage. According to the Gospel of Luke:

> The Spirit of the Lord is upon me, because he hath anointed me to preach the gospel to the poor; he hath sent me to heal the brokenhearted, to preach deliverance to the captives, and recovering of sight to the blind, to set at liberty them that are bruised,
>
> —Luke 4:18 (KJV)

As horrible as parts of my life have been, God has flipped the script! The Spirit of the Lord favors me, and I am empowered to set free the captives of addictions! *From Crack to Christ: Twenty Years Later* provides practical lessons of how to accomplish just that.

After 28-years of drug and alcohol indulgence (even longer for tobacco), I had an encounter with a Savior! I never spent one day in rehab or participated in any 12-step program. I did, however, take one step to Jesus, and Jesus stepped to me, delivering me instantly!

Thirteen years after my deliverance, the Lord led my matriculation to the prestigious Samuel Dewitt Proctor School of Theology at Virginia Union University. Without a bachelor's degree, I enrolled in a master's degree program while working full-time, taking my courses nights and weekends. Four years later, I'd earned two master's degrees: a Master of Divinity and a Master of Arts in Christian Education. I then took a few months off and enrolled in a doctoral program at the highly acclaimed Regent University. In the spring of 2019, I became the first doctor in our family, earning a Doctoral Degree in Strategic Leadership with a concentration in healthcare leadership. It is only due to God's grace and miraculous power that I've been able to achieve these accomplishments.

In the movie *Brian Banks*, there is the profound quote: "The only thing you can control in life is how you respond to it." Despite what I've been through, no story is as compelling or as transformative as God's story. My story is just a minuscule portion of His. Humbly, my heartfelt desire is that *From Crack to Christ: Twenty Years Later* assists someone else in embracing the miracle-working power found in the greatest story ever told. I faithfully believe that they too may transition from crack (or any other addiction) to a loving Christ!

So, be well, be in health, stay safe, and prosper!

In spirit and truth,
Dr. Stephen B. Towns, Sr.

LOST

CHAPTER 1:
I WAS DEEP IN SIN

There I was driving down Meadow Street. I'd just finished smoking a fat jumbo. That's a marijuana cigarette loaded with crack cocaine, for those of you that don't know. My heart was pounding and my brain was fried. I could feel my pulse slowing down. With each slowed heartbeat, everything became darker. There was no doubt that I was about to black out. My palms became sweaty, and my grip on the steering wheel loosened as I began to surrender control of the car. I felt as if I were sinking inside of myself.

I swerved to avoid sideswiping a car on the narrow street. I was a breath away from a catastrophe. Just then, I did something that I'd never done before. At the time, I had no idea why I was doing it. Looking back, I believe that my heart was about to burst! Yet, something inside of me cried out! It was almost as if there was someone else living in my rapidly decaying body. Helplessly, almost subconsciously, I witnessed my soul cry out as I then yelled aloud, "JESUS!"

I don't know why or how it happened, but instantly I became sober. It was as if I had never smoked hundreds of dollars worth of crack cocaine over the past 48 hours.

Suddenly, I realized there was something else transpiring. As I eased my car into park in front of my in-laws' house, where my family and I were staying while we saved money for our own home, a realization struck me like a youthful Mike Tyson body shot! There was no more anxiety. There was no more fear. A sense of calm engulfed me. I got a foretaste of something I never knew, beyond my immediate comprehension; it became apparent that I was at peace.

The Lord had spared me from an accident. He'd spared me from possible jail time because I was as dirty as a preschooler's mud pie. I believe He spared me from a massive heart attack and possible death! Only God knows what was about to happen to me. Feeling grateful to be alive, I went inside the house. I told myself that this was it! No more drugs! I had enough sense to know that I was saved by divine intervention, and this time, I'd quit using once and for all.

I told myself that this time would be different. This was the time that I would get myself together. But how many dope fiends or former addicts or loved ones of addicts reading this know that just a few days later I was getting high again?

But where did all this madness begin? What led such a promising youth to such a predictable demise? Well, let's see... I did have all the societal accepted excuses. Yeah, you could say that I was underprivileged, from a broken home, the product of mean inner-city streets. Yeah, you could also note that there were the hereditary curses of adultery, alcoholism, and vicious spankings with extension cords and a host of other whelp-raising things.

If I were looking for a place to lay blame, I might point out that my parents shared the sin of omission: neglecting to embrace that which those who raised them had taught them about the God of their elders' salvation. Yeah, that sounds really good, but the reality is that no matter what the cause, I know that this account is not about affixing blame to any person.

My mother and father were both teenagers when they married, and I believe that at the time they both always thought that they were doing what was best for my brother and me. I reflect now only because I've learned that someone else may be saved by this testimony. Many of us need to realize that no matter what situation or circumstances that we find ourselves in, Christ specializes in reversing the curse.

All God wants to know is, will we be made whole? If we learn to worship Him in spirit and in truth, then He will provide all our needs. But I was lost in a microwave society of increasing sin where casual sex, violence, and drugs were infused in the very fabric of my world.

THE CHILDHOOD

I was born and raised in the slums of Trenton, New Jersey. The only homes I remembered were in the projects. Back then, the projects was a step up for most blacks that migrated north from southern States, and everybody was trying to get into the "PJ's". The Lincoln Homes at 177 Old Rose Street is where I was street-hardened for life.

When Martin Luther King, Jr. was assassinated in 1968, my brother and I, at twelve and eleven years old, were coming home from the movies and literally got caught in the middle of the riots that ensued. We witnessed hate-incensed policemen unleashing attack dogs on crowds of demonstrators. We witnessed our neighbors looting businesses and running down the street with sofas on their backs. We witnessed military tanks rumbling through our neighborhood with machine-gunners posted on top of them.

I believe my mother was traumatized and definitely had seen enough of Trenton. She decided it was time to move, so to the suburbs we went. My mother, brother and I moved to the yuppie-rich town of Princeton, New Jersey. In fact, the town was so financially well off that most of the white kids and half of the blacks literally had money to burn, and up in smoke it went. Soon I was introduced to marijuana and hashish. It was there that at twelve years old I got high for the first time. Princeton is only 15 miles north of Trenton, but believe me, it was another world!

I found out that there was more around than marijuana. The year was 1970, and everyone drank beer or Boones Farm, Yago, MD 20-20, Wild Irish Rose, or Thunderbird wines. As a high school freshman, while maintaining a "straight A" average, I experimented with tripping off on hallucinogenic acid on the weekends.

All the so-called bad boys were shooting heroin though. My brother, whom I believe yearned for acceptance, found a friend in the mighty white horse. I had always been afraid of needles. In fact, the doctor had to catch me to give me one. And now these fools were injecting themselves! I knew they were crazy! It seemed like everyone in the hood was doing some type of drugs! The Vietnam War was coming to a close, and getting high was truly an acceptable sign of the times.

My main crew, which consisted of an eclectic circle of primarily slightly younger friends, escaped through sports. We mainly drank beer and smoked and sold refer. Sports were in my blood. My dad had played semi-pro football and baseball. Although I was often the smallest one in the mix, I had the heart of a lion and nerves of steel.

I played every sport there was, but basketball was my true love. Every day I lived on the basketball court. I came from football practice and played basketball. I came from baseball practice and played basketball. When it snowed, my crew and I would shovel the snow off the entire court so that we could play basketball.

In high school I became a star, and my brother, who was easily more intelligent than I, became strung out! My mother, who often worked two and three jobs, just to provide our essentials, didn't have a clue, bless her heart. Although it repulsed me, I kept his secret. It wasn't until his senior year, when he contracted and nearly gave my mother and me hepatitis, that his secret was finally out of the bag.

I began to sink deeper in sin. For years, the Lord rebuked the hand of death from me, as I foolishly became a ghetto legend in the infamous underworld of drugs, violence, and sex. When I was sixteen, I was stabbed in the head with a broken coke bottle. That same weekend, while the stitches were still wet, a policeman whose son I had punched in the face a few months earlier marked me for death.

His son and I had made friends days after the incident, but his father held a grudge. As an off-duty policeman, he'd come to my school the following Monday in a sweat suit and tried to bait me, all 130 pounds of me, into a fight. This was a grown man, a police officer, over six feet tall and weighing well over two hundred pounds, trying to pick a fight with me, a short but lean 16-year-old punk junior in high school.

I was scared, but I didn't show it. I remembered my father telling me that this man was soft when they were in high school, so I took his heart by telling him to go and get his punk-*** son and I'd go and get my father, and then we could settle this once and for all. He pondered my suggestion, and then he quickly left me alone and jetted from the school.

Now, several months later, while at a backyard party at their house, I was singled out and attacked by a soldier who, I found out later, had been brought in town to teach me a lesson. A true mercenary, I guess. After being confronted by this maniac and not backing down, I turned to walk away and was struck with a club and knocked unconscious. Miraculously, I got my hand up before the club struck me in the face, yet the force was so strong that it fractured my hand and then caught me in the jaw and still had enough force to knock me out. It was simply the grace of God that the blow didn't catch me flush in the head, where I still had the stitches from the stab wound.

RUNNING WITH THE BIG DOGS

I was the youngest one in my family of cousins and I began to hang out with guys older than myself. It wasn't long before I was introduced to cocaine. As a baby-faced 17-year-old, I now hung out with twenty-year-old thugs in Princeton and my cousins in Trenton. This, coupled with my basketball notoriety, made me known at all the after-hour hot spots in central Jersey.

Despite all the distractions though, the Lord was keeping me even then. I graduated from high school in the upper portion of my class. I had a couple of scholarship offers to go and play basketball, but because I was chasing the skirts, as my dad always called it, I took several thousand dollars in scholarship money and opted for a local community college to stay near my high school sweetheart.

When the college's basketball coach left over the summer to coach professionally in Italy and the new coach unfairly cut me from the team (even though I dominated the try-out sessions), I turned to selling "Acapulco Gold" marijuana on campus. Again, I was a star. I hung out in the lounge practically all day, shooting pool and gambling, playing blackjack. I had two choice honeys and was the top balling intramural player on campus. After the next semester I got bored and dropped out of school.

After several years of accelerated chaos, at 21 years old I left New Jersey. Against my parents' wishes, with $200 in my pocket, I moved 300 miles away to Virginia. It took me less than a week to find a job, and I began selling clothes in the hottest, number one urban-fashion store in the heart of the Confederacy. It wasn't long before I was supplying cocaine to all my friends and coworkers. I had juice! I had power! Everybody gave me my props!

I was the man!

Soon I had a son, and three years later, I married his mother. I never left the fast lane though. I continued to keep company with murderers and thieves. I regularly frequented some of the most cutthroat spots in the city. At that time, the Richmond gangsters proudly wore the infamous crown of the "per capita murder capital of America" and it's only by the grace of God that I wasn't murdered or was forced to commit murder myself. I carried two pistols wherever I went, and I didn't even go to the bathroom in my own house unless I was strapped.

In the months that ensued, I began running between Virginia and New York three to four times a month, bringing back ounces of powder cocaine. I remember hitting the Richmond Trailways bus station on the Boulevard about 5 a.m. one Saturday morning. I had just come off a run and carried a shoulder bag that contained enough coke to send me to prison for fifty years. When I strolled into the empty station, my eyes scanned the terminal. Then I saw him, just as he saw me. It was a policeman down by the main entrance. He and I were the only ones in the terminal. This was not good. My street sense knew this was trouble, and my blood began to boil.

My eyes were frozen on him as he looked up on the wall to see what bus I'd just come in on. He saw it said New York. I'm sure his gut told him that I was dirty. He started walking briskly towards me. My first reaction was to run back out the side door to the unloading area where I'd come from. But something told me to stay cool and keep walking.

As we approached each other, we were now close enough to see the color of each other's eyes. As he stared in my face, I stayed cool. I slowly and cockily looked away and kept strolling. No one else was in the station, yet the policeman walked right at me and slightly brushed my shoulder as I strutted right past him and out the door into a taxi. He tried to make me panic, but I didn't bite. Phew!

On the outside I was as cool as they come—stupid but cool. However, on the inside I was about to wet my pants! That was the last drug run I ever made. After that, I tried sending my main partner as a mule in my place, but he proved that even he couldn't be trusted.

GOD WAS TRYING TO GET MY ATTENTION

I have no doubt that though I was unsaved and deep in sin, God was looking out for my foolish self even then. Having all power in His hands, God knew the plans that He had for my life. God knew that I'd be sharing this testimony with you on this day! He knew then what I've come to know now: that God keeps us in spite of all our shortcomings; in spite of our slothfulness; in spite of our disobedience. In time I came to realize that God doesn't deal with us after our sins nor rewards us according to our mistakes.

Unfortunately for me, I had to endure more trials and tribulations before I realized God was trying to get my attention. Drugs fueled my pursuit for abundance and greed. I fell victim to the urban legend that the larger you lived, the bigger a man you were. So, I had to have more drugs, more money, more women, consume more food, and own and wear more fresh gear. Everything was more, and more was better. I juggled three 21-year-old girlfriends in addition to satisfying my wife. I slept with each of them at least once a week. The really scary thing, to me, was that they were all content!

I, myself, however, was a different story. I was unhappy and yearned for something real, something true. God was gently tugging at my heart, yet I knew Him not. Excessiveness continued to consume me, and I allowed this lifestyle to destroy my marriage and cause me to abandon my best friend, my four-year-old son.

My intent is not to glorify myself or the devil or the lifestyle that I had. My sole purpose is to touch someone that can relate to where I'm coming from. To let you know that if the Lord could deliver a wretch like me, then He can also deliver any of you. That's what the Bible means when it says that the Lord "is no respecter of persons" (Acts 10:34, KJV). He loves us all unconditionally, and if you give Him a chance, He will reveal that love to you.

I found out though that the choices in life that we make all carry consequences, and some of the prices that we pay are often more severe than we realize. In retrospect, of everyone that I knew in the drug game, from New York to Florida to California, not one of them that stayed in the game had a happy ending. Not one! All us paid a heavy price. Some of them became murderers headed for hell, others were gunned down and went to hell, and others still died from overdoses and burn in hell. Some were at home in a living hell, but it didn't stop there.

If nothing happened to them, then it was someone that they loved, possibly someone guilty only by association. Maybe their innocent brother was gunned down or their children faced some untimely affliction or death. Maybe their baby sister hung out, became strung out, and got turned out. The point I'm trying to make is that there is a price to be paid for forcing bondage and hardship on God's beloved people. And when you sell drugs, that's exactly what you are doing! You are invariably forcing pain and hardship on God's people! One of the biggest prices that I paid was suffering through my own addiction!

In addition to that, my beautiful 21-year-old stepsister, who lived in Trenton, supposedly committed suicide. I had just seen her weeks before at our grandfather's funeral, and she told me that there was too much drama in her life. She asked me if she and her young son could come and stay with me in Virginia.

I was a 28-year-old homeowner and living large. I told her that I would love for her to come and stay with me, but that I was leaving the next day, which was Sunday. She told me that she had some business to take care of that coming Monday morning, and she begged me to wait for her. I reasoned that I had a rented car and that I had to be back to work that same Monday morning. I told her to simply get on a Greyhound and that everything would be OK. She grudgingly agreed. I never heard from her or saw her alive again. I left the next day, and a few weeks later, I got word that she had hung herself.

When you live deep in sin and sow the devil's seeds of discord, it's like throwing a demonic pebble in a fire and brimstone pond, and you have no idea how far Satan's ripples are going to reach.

CHAPTER 2:
GOD FLIPPED THE SCRIPT

As time passed, I remained in this vicious spiral of self-destruction. I remarried and had a five-year old daughter. My wife was raised a Pentecostal, in the Church of God in Christ, which she introduced me to. I went to church sometimes, and sometimes my wife and I left church and went to the clubs. Because of my true love and respect for her, I never wanted to expose her to the drug life. It wasn't as if I had a secret life; it was simply that I was shielding her from that damning lifestyle. Most of my friends involved their girls in the life, and after time, these once beautiful females looked used, elderly, and shriveled up. I knew I didn't want that for my wife, so I eventually stopped selling drugs and began a career in the computer industry, but I still used drugs heavily.

In addition to God's grace, it took the prayers of many not to give up on me. For you see, I knew that church is where I belonged, but even after I first joined, I went back on the devil's territory. I thought that I could straddle the fence and get high on Friday and Saturday and then sometimes come to church on

Sunday. I was convinced that I could handle being a weekend addict, but the devil had a trap set.

This time my adversary assigned seven more powerfully addicting spirits to cut me off from the church and kill me. There was a deep and intricate trap set, but God flipped the script, and what was meant for my harm turned out to be for my good!

My deliverance was imminent. It began by my pastor laying his hands on the belly of my wife, who was around seven months pregnant with our second daughter. I vividly remember the pastor saying that this unborn child would not fall prey to the hereditary curses that plagued the others. When he said that, my mind flashed to the time when my wife was upset because I had been out all night smoking crack and I came home to find my clothes thrown outside and the deadbolt lock on the door. As I pleaded with her to open the door, which she eventually did, I remember my daughter Kelli, at the time four years old, standing there crying, asking. "Mommy, why are you doing that to Daddy?"

That incident pricked my heart, because it showed me just how much my daughter still loved me. She had no idea of the mess that I was in or how much suffering I was inflicting on my family, and she didn't care. That was my first awareness of the agape love of Christ.

Despite all my shortcomings, despite all my sins, my daughter still loved me. What true and unconditional love that is. The revelation was, that's how God's love is! Even though we fall and may be in the midst of our mess, He still loves us and gives us the opportunity to get up and go on! God gives us the strength to resume our walk and continue our journey on the path of righteousness.

Now the Lord was using my unborn child and my sincere love for it to convict me in my spirit. When nothing else had worked, not the sincere love and desires of those closest to me or the common sense and basic instinct of self-preservation, the Lord chose my unborn child to speak to my heart.

THE DEVIL INTENSIFIED HIS PLOT TO KILL ME

Shortly after that, I was sober and sitting at home, in our new tri-level, around 8 p.m. on a Friday night, watching the Knicks on cable. I was fixing some French fries on the mid-level when the smoke alarm went off. *What in the world?*, I thought. I raced upstairs and the kitchen was filling with smoke coming from the pot with hot grease. I moved the pot off the stove, and the sudden breeze must've caused it to ignite! Flames were shooting everywhere! Like a fool, I threw a glass of water on it! The flames shot up the wall and covered the whole ceiling!

Just then my wife came downstairs to see why I was calling her name with such urgency! When she saw that fire, her first reaction was to run outside! As she headed for the door, she realized that all she had on was that BIG maternity underwear that pregnant women wear! (Forgive me, dear; I love you!) Also, our daughter Kelli was upstairs asleep!

I grabbed the flaming pot to move it away from the curtains. It began splashing all over my hands! I couldn't let go. I headed for the front door, but something said, don't go that way. I came back to the kitchen. Had I tripped along the way, the flames would've trapped the whole family upstairs. Later, the fireman told me that if I had opened the front door with the flaming pot, then the breeze probably would have caused the flames to engulf me. But look at God's mercy!

I know now that the enemy was trying to kill me, my family, and especially the unborn child. I screamed for my wife to give me a towel, and frantically I began to battle those flames as she called 911!

At that moment, I didn't have the sense to simply cover the pot and smother the fire. Finally, all the flames were gone. The flames had shot through the stove's range hood and knocked out all the power in the house. I got everyone outside. It was then that I realized that the fire and hot grease had burned all the skin off my right hand. Excruciating pain tapped me on the shoulder. I began to curse like a drunken sailor.

The firemen arrived, took one look at my hand, and called an ambulance to take me to the hospital. They told my wife that they were taking me to the Medical College of Virginia (where I worked) Burn Unit. I know that the enemy was mad that my family was out of danger, so he made an all-out effort to get me. On the way to the hospital, my pulse dropped down to 40 and I lost consciousness and began to go into shock. Although I wasn't high that night, it was only because I was broke from smoking up all that my money could buy the three days prior and all my credit sources had cut me off.

While unconscious, I felt the devil trying to choke the life out of me. There's no doubt in my mind that I was dying. Again, in my spirit, I cried unto the Lord, and I pleaded, "Lord! Please, I don't want to die. I haven't even seen my little baby girl yet! Don't let her grow up without her father!"

Clearly, in a mighty voice, the Spirit of the Lord spoke to me and told me that I would live and not die! The Lord said to rest assured, that not only would I see the birth of this blessed child, but I would be around to raise her properly!

Just then I heard someone calling my name. "Stephen, wake up! Wake up! Stephen, if you can hear me, squeeze my hand!"

It was the paramedic. I opened my eyes. She screamed at me, "Don't you ever scare me like that again!"

I'd come so close to death that the ambulance detoured and took me to the nearest hospital. They were afraid that I wasn't going to make it to MCV, which had a specialized Burn/Trauma unit.

Once more, the Lord's grace and mercy was extended unto me. The Lord was again trying to get my attention! I believe He allowed these events to happen—not to kill me, but to begin to fulfill His will for my life. I beg all that are reading this book: if you're living in sin, don't be as hardheaded as I was. Don't make the Lord give you near-death Jonah experiences in order to get through to you! Save yourself and your loved ones some pain, suffering, and hardship.

GETTING MY PRIORITIES IN ORDER

When I remarried, I also began officiating high school basketball. I became so engrossed with it that I placed my officiating above everything else in my life. My family, my job, and even God! The trip part is that I loved the game of basketball so much that I cared more about it than I did about myself. Invariably, I never used drugs while officiating, but when the games were over, I rarely went straight home either. The devil tricked me into believing that it was OK because I needed to relax and wind down after my games.

But again, God didn't reward me according to my iniquities or deal with me according to my sins! But this time, it took me suffering through paralysis in my right arm for over a month and spinal laser-surgery where I was given a 1 in 200 chance to ever walk again! If the surgery had not been successful and I had to spend the rest of my life in a wheelchair, it would certainly have been what I deserved for all the pain and suffering that my life had caused so many others. But look at God! Instead, He didn't look at what I could do for Him, but He showed me what He could do for me!

He planted me in a ministry where I could be spiritually fed and grow. I began to eat His Word, and I began learning more and more about Him. I developed a balance in my life. I restructured and made Christ the number one priority in my life. My family came next, then my job, and my officiating dropped down to fourth. Instantly, my officiating took off to new heights, and now, in addition to high school officiating, I work on the semi-professional level as well.

Unfortunately, before I got to that point, I backslid (suffered setbacks) a few more times, and it wasn't until later, while in service on a Sunday night, that my miracle manifested itself. The sermon that night pricked my heart and hit me like a sledge-hammer. Through my tears, I called out to the Lord from the depths of my heart. I said, "Father, despite everything You've already done for me, I still don't know if You are real or not. I have never honestly tried You, Lord, with all my heart. But Father, I'm sick and tired of being sick and tired, and tonight I'm giving You my all! Tonight, Lord, like never before, I am surrendering my all to You. Lord, do a new thing in me. Lord, if You are who You say You are, please take all this madness away!"

MY TEST FOR DELIVERANCE

That night I went home and went straight to bed, which was unusual for me. Around 1 a.m. the phone rang, and it was the brother of a drug dealer friend of mine. He asked what I was doing and said that he was right around the corner, headed to my house, with kilos of cocaine. You must realize that I lived over 15 miles outside of the city, and there was no reason for him to just happen to be in my vicinity. He said that if I got up and let him come over, I could snort, smoke, or stash as much cocaine as I wanted! For a moment, my mind raced, my palms got sweaty, and I began salivating! I anticipated what he just told me and what it meant! Just the thought of doing all those drugs triggered a chemical imbalance in my brain! Normally when this happened, I had to have it!

Then the Holy Ghost brought to my remembrance my plea to God earlier that night. I then uncharacteristically played it off and told the brother on the phone that I appreciated the offer, but that I was returning to work tomorrow after being out 8 weeks from my burned hand, and that maybe I would call him when I got off work.

The brother on the phone asked in disbelief, "Is this Steve? Am I talking to Steve? Nigger, what's wrong with you?" I smiled to myself and said not a word.

Friends, that was July 1996, and I haven't called him back yet! That night I passed my test, and through my sincerity and faithfulness, the Lord delivered me instantly from cigarettes, alcohol, and drugs, and I haven't touched any of them since! I've never been in a 12-step program. I just took ONE STEP TOWARDS JESUS, and Jesus stepped to me! He loosed my shackles and set me free!

You see, God had to deliver me from tobacco, alcohol, and drugs all at once, because for me my addictions had become progressive. If I smoked a cigarette, I wanted a beer. If I drank a beer, I wanted to smoke a joint. If I smoked a joint, then I had to make it a jumbo. And once I started with the Jums, then it was straight back to Crack City!

But look at God: through His grace and mercy, He washed me whiter than snow! The truly great thing about it is that God really has no respect of persons! If He did it for me, then He can do it for you also! All you need to do is to believe, receive, and separate yourself from your sinful environment, keep the company of those who are spiritually stronger than you, pray without ceasing, and feed yourself on the Word of God. Then stand back and watch God move!

Now I'm the one that my family calls to get a prayer through! The Lord heard my prayers and healed my 69-year-old aunt of breast cancer without surgery or treatment. Now it's I that the Lord uses to minister to my grandmother, who was the only one in church when I was a child. The Lord uses little old me. The ex-drug dealer, the ex-adulterer, the ex-addict!

I take no credit for myself, but forever I'll shout TO GOD BE THE GLORY FOR EVER AND EVER, FOR THE GREAT THINGS THAT HE HAS DONE! HIS NAME IS WORTHY TO BE PRAISED!

Know this, God can deliver you in an instant, but I believe that it takes a lifetime to sustain your deliverance. This race called life is not given to the swift. I encourage you to read on as I share the holy lessons I have learned that continue to take me "From Crack To Christ."

CHAPTER 3:

LOOKING FOR LOVE IN ALL THE WRONG PLACES

I want to deal with the love factor next, because after being delivered from drugs, I found that residual addiction issues became another huge hurdle to overcome. I had to overcome the fear and realization of the fact that I thought that I could not perform sexually without being high. Hello, somebody! I'm being real here and exposing the devil for the trickster that he is!

I need to get raw with you because many men have tried to go straight and give up drugs only to find that they no longer contained the sexual prowess that they once had. If the truth were told, many men may grudgingly admit that they have rushed back to using drugs solely for this reason.

Men will also find that by discontinuing their extended drug use, they are throwing away the subliminal crutch they had leaned on for so long. To get even deeper, oftentimes the chemical imbalance that the male's body is now undergoing, coupled with the fear of insecurity, will force them to frequently suffer through impotence and possibly even the appearance of the shrinking of their genitals.

My brothers, if you think this is bad, it can and often does get worse because our women may begin to complain when there is a drastic change in our sexual performance. The worst thing that the woman can do during this period is to cruelly verbalize their displeasure in not being satisfied by their mate. I thank God for anointing me to shame the devil by revealing a part of this intricate plot to keep people in bondage.

I would be remiss if I didn't state that the Bible says that premarital sex is a sin. Additionally, if you are a new, born-again creature, then the enemy may also attempt to spiritually black-mail you into believing that God knows all the times that you were 'in between the sheets' and then keep you ashamed of your previous behavior. If Satan can get you to dwell on your sinful past, then he can continually entice you with today's pleasures of carnality and your lustful gratification, blinding you to the promise of your purpose.

He will even go so far as to avail to you those types of the opposite (or same) sex that you previously dreamed about enjoying. Hello, somebody! If you are a man that prefers short and shapely women, then the enemy will not send you tall, skinny ones. If you are a woman who previously couldn't resist certain situations, then you can rest assured that those same irresistible situations are vastly approaching.

We must understand that all too often the bondage of sexual and drug addictions go together as compatibly as peanut butter and jelly. The only way that we can successfully overcome them totally is if we turn them completely over to the Lord. Once we do that, then God will empower us to resist every enticement and truly live a victorious life. Psalm 34:19 (KJV) says that: *Many are the afflictions of the righteous: but the LORD delivereth him out of them all.*

Married couples must understand and supportively work through these residual issues of drug addiction and abuse. If you endure together, then they will pass. I personally had to go back to my square one to fully understand and conquer my dilemma. My ground zero was my relationship with and faith in God. After cherishing that fact, God began to reveal to me how a hereditary curse of feeling neglected ultimately contributed to me looking for love in all the wrong places. I had to decipher: *just what is this thing called Love?*

Love, by all accounts, is a wonderful feeling. When people think of love, they often imagine Cupid flying around with a bow and arrow, choosing targets at random, and causing those struck by his arrows to immediately go gaga and start thinking about the birds and the bees. There is even a holiday created to symbolize the feeling of love. And, fellas, we'd better not forget that special day in February when we are all expected to buy flowers, candy, and even diamonds and furs—Valentine's Day.

The feeling of love is something that everyone in the world wants. It's something that everyone in the world desires. And it's certainly something that every living creature in the world needs.

But are we looking for love in all the wrong places?

When people feel that they are not loved, then they open themselves up to feelings of worthlessness, guilt, and even suicide. Whether you know it or not, these feelings are driven by demonic spirits. Once we begin to embrace any of those spirits, they will begin to dominate our thoughts, and if we're not watchful, those spirits may even overpower our spiritual, mental, and emotional stability.

Most drug abusers are lost from the Gospel and find themselves deprived of true love. Consequently, people will attempt to manufacture that which they believe they need. Some turn, as I did, to sex. Seeing just how many females we can acquire, satisfy, and use. My running partners and I used to have contests to see just how many women we could have sex within a day or a week.

There are those that may find themselves experimenting with homosexuality and lesbianism. Others may find themselves in one abusive relationship after another. Many turn to alcohol and drugs and/or various combinations of the above. Still, there are those that begin embracing deviant sexual or violent behavior such as child molestation and/or rape. Please understand that demonic spirits exist and skillfully fuel these actions.

My drug addiction inevitably clouded my ability to separate reality from illusion, and an insatiable craving of lust pacified my natural desire for love. Because I was looking for love in all the wrong places, I became as predictable as nightfall and as controllable, to familiar spirits, as a light switch.

Familiar spirits are those demonic spirits that have been with us so long and know us so well that they can and do push our buttons at their discretion to achieve the results that they desire. Familiar spirits can be in our families for generations and have little difficulty in manipulating us to the extent of gradually destroying our lives by committing horrendous crimes to ourselves and loved ones and others.

I had to defeat a familiar spirit that had coerced me to use drugs every time my wife said something I didn't like. Rather than have a knock-down-drag-out confrontation with her (or so I convinced myself), I dealt with that stress by just leaving the house and going and getting high. So, what my familiar spirit would do was predictably push my button by getting my wife to say something that I didn't like.

I eventually had to disconnect that demonic button by practicing James 4:7 which says to resist the devil and he will flee from you. As simple as this sounds, it works! Once you begin to render the devil's buttons useless, you begin to break the chains of bondage and transfer control of your life back to God, where it was intended to be all along.

It is a natural principal that whatever we feed will become stronger. Circumspectly, there is nothing in this world set up to assist the believer in living holy. If you continually watch sexually suggestive shows on television or even commercials and sports programs, those connotations will become imbedded within you. Then, if you fail to pray, read your Bible, or go to church to hear from a man after God's own heart, then how will your spirit man survive? The answer is, it cannot!

It is a fact that we are all spirit-driven, and if we are not being led by God's Spirit, then whose spirit is influencing us? There is nothing that transpires on Earth that does not have spiritual significance. When you begin to mature in Christendom, you will grow into the understanding of spiritual warfare. The battle is for your heart and soul and frequently takes place in the battle-field of your mind. The outcome may transpire into life-altering decisions and repercussions for not just you but, inescapably, for your generations to come.

That might be too deep for some of you right now, so let's continue to take a look at how the Bible defines the word *love*. The word in Hebrew which is translated as meaning 'God's love' is *ahabah*. In Greek, it's *agape*. In *Smith's Bible Dictionary*, love is described as: A spiritual affection for holy things which is a fruit of the Spirit, opposed to all evil, and only satisfied with a likeness to Jesus Christ and God.

A SPIRITUAL AFFECTION FOR HOLY THINGS

This means that our pursuit for love should not be on the Internet, in the malls, at the health club, or even in church. Hello, somebody. But we should set our spiritual affection for spiritual things. That means that we should live by Matthew 6:33 that says that we should seek first the Kingdom of God, and His righteousness, and then all these things shall be added unto us. Certainly, one of those things is LOVE!

I had to learn—and am still learning—that, as men, once we set our affections on spiritual things and begin walking after the Spirit and not lusting after the flesh, then God will allow us to find that special woman, that good thing, and enjoy her and experience love as God intended. Remember that God created Eve from Adam's rib and intends for married couples to be bone of each other's bone and flesh of each other's flesh. When your wife is truly your 'helpmeet', one of the things she does is to 'help meet' your need for sexual gratification and companionship.

Most men fail to realize that until their vertical relationship with God is intact, none of the horizontal relationships in our lives will prosper! A lot of men will continue to get caught up as I did and see women as sexual objects designed for one purpose, which is solely to satisfy, not help meet, our needs.

Let's revisit our Biblical definition and note where we were instructed to be: *opposed to all evil, and only satisfied with a likeness to Jesus Christ and God*. Being opposed to all evil means that our motives must be pure. We should not be driven by lust in our pursuit for love. We should not have an eye for our neighbor's wife, even though she is pursuing us like a tigress as Potiphar's wife pursued and eventually cornered Joseph.

We men must not confuse our ease in pulling women with being a gift from God when, in reality, it is a curse from hell. I have never had a problem in getting women and so even now I must die daily in my flesh in order to not be overtaken by the familiar spirits that desire to sidetrack and distract me from the destiny that God has ordained for my life.

But how can we have our desire for love satisfied only with a likeness to Jesus Christ and God? Well, we've got to seek His presence and stay before Him. We've got to thirst after righteousness for righteousness' sake. We've got to realize that our desire to love and be loved is natural but also not fail to realize what is that imbedded in our nature—causing us to seek love—are our basic spiritual instincts to seek, love, and worship our Creator. When we don't understand that as a natural component of our being, then our affection ultimately becomes misguided: we truly begin an insatiable cycle of seeking to find love in all the wrong places and suffering devastating consequences.

Please read First John 4:7-21. This expounds on the source of love. It teaches us that God loved us so much that He sent, and ultimately sacrificed, His one and only Son so that you and I could live eternally through Him. We learn through this text that God *is* love, and that He first loved us even before we loved ourselves.

That is so profound and powerful, yet simple and basic. God loves us so much that when we believe and embrace Him, He forgives us for all our sins. We and our slates are miraculously washed clean. Our sins are thrown into the sea of forgetfulness! God commands us to love one another the way that Christ first loved us. Unconditionally! There is no greater love!

Once we learn this about the Most High God, I believe that we should celebrate the ultimate love day, not in February, but on Good Friday. For you see, no greater display of love has ever been shown than on that day. On that day, the fulfillment of the greatest love story ever imagined took place. That was the day when Jesus died for our sins and paid the ultimate and final price for our atonement. On that day, a debt was paid by one that didn't owe it. On that day, a debt was erased that we could never pay. That was the day when the greatest gift of love ever was given to all mankind. That was the day when what Satan thought was meant for our demise turned out to be for our victorious good.

When we are lost in the darkness of bondage, we continuously look for love in all the wrong places. Once we are found though, and are shown the light, we must not forget that the Bible tells us that we are *in* this world but not *of* this world. We must thirst for a spiritual affection for holy things. We must be opposed to all evil things, and our need for love must only be satisfied with a likeness to Jesus Christ and God.

I had to learn that love cannot be found on the plush leather seats of an SUV. Love cannot be fulfilled on a loveseat or sofa while your mother is at work. Love is not obtained through a one-night stand at the Motel 6. And, brothers, it surely will not last when it is found when thinking with your smaller head. Hello! Have you been looking for love in all the wrong places?

If you're looking for love in all the wrong places, then you don't know that love is both an attribute of God and a description of His being. He alone is the epitome of divine love and the source of all true love. His love is unconditional and consistently seeks the highest good of the one who is loved.

You see, some balladeer's singing has ill-programmed this world with the lyrics, "You're nobody till somebody loves you; you're nobody till somebody cares."

The truth is we must know with the very fabric of our being that even if no one else loves us, it really doesn't matter, because our Creator loves us, and there is no greater love than the love of one willing to lay down their life for another.

Please understand that love is not only one of God's attributes; it is also a part of His nature. The Bible declares that God is Love! He is the personification of perfect love. Paul's letter to the Ephesians said that only His love surpasses our powers of understanding. [Eph. 3:19] Jeremiah said that love like this is everlasting! [Jer. 31:3] Hosea said, "He'll love you freely." [Hos. 14:4] And the Apostle John wrote that His love is sacrificial and enduring till the end. [Jn. 3:16;13] First John 3:16 (KJV) states: "For God so loved the world, that He gave His only begotten Son, that whosoever believeth in Him, should not perish, but have everlasting life."

People, we should all desire to have everlasting life! I had to learn not to look for love in all the wrong places. I had to learn not to desire the love and approval of man—my so-called friends, classmates, relatives, teammates, or coworkers. It's wonderful if everyone loves you, but even if nobody loves me, I might have to cry sometimes, but I will be all right, because I know that God loves me and He will never leave me nor forsake me.

Even when I mess up and come up short of His glory, like everyone has, I know that He's there with outstretched arms, saying, "Come unto me for my yoke is easy, and my burden is light." (Matthew 11:30, KJV) Even in the midst of sin, be it sins of omission (failing to do that which I know is right) or sins of commission (doing what I know is wrong), I still have the love of the Savior.

God loved me enough to send down, from glory, His only son and extend to me new mercies day by day. STOP THE PRESS! Did you hear what I said? You must know that every single day that God's grace allows us to wake up, God extends, to us, new mercy! Daily! Phew, that's love!

God's Son, Jesus, loved me enough to stretch out His arms and die for my sins, covering me in His precious blood. And the Holy Spirit loves me enough to strengthen me, to be a present help in my time of need, to be a Comforter in the midnight hour, a guide on the path of salvation to fulfill my destination of a heavenly home. I've learned not to look for love in all the wrong places!

You see, true Christian love is a fruit of the Spirit of Jesus in the believer. Ephesians 5:2 says that God commands us to walk in love, as Christ also loved us, and has given Himself for us as an offering and a sacrifice.

Love is like oil to the wheels of obedience. David tells us in Psalm 119:32 that it enables us to run the way of God's commandments. Paul's first letter to the Corinthian church (First Corinthians 13:3,8) warned that without such love, we are nothing. God's Spirit-inspired love never fails but always flourishes.

Why settle for a feeling when you can embrace God's Spirit? Why continue to look for love in all the wrong places? Why live outside the door when His word says, "Knock, and it shall be opened. Ask and ye shall receive." (Matthew 7:7–8)

God's love is purer and more rewarding than any drug could ever be. You don't have to pawn your wedding ring to buy it, for it's absolutely free! You will never wake up with a hangover. You won't have to degrade yourself by doing "things-for-things" to enjoy it! You will never wonder if the lover of your soul will still love you in the morning. Most importantly, I guarantee you that when you call, God will never look at His caller ID and then fail to answer you.

Once you embrace the love of the Savior, you will realize that you have been looking for love in all the wrong places. Once you experience the lover of your soul, you will no longer be able to accept any substitutes.

It's then that you'll understand why God said that "he that puts mother or father or son or daughter above Me is not worthy of Me." (Matthew 10:37). It's because there is no greater love that you can ever know than the love of Christ Jesus. And once you begin to walk in that love, you will never again search for love. Love will abound all around you, for God *is* love. [1 Jn. 4:8]

CHAPTER 4:

WHEN YOU'RE A SKUNK, YOU CAN'T SMELL THE STINK

Do any of you remember the cartoon featuring the amorous French skunk Pepe Le Pew? Pepe's love affection was a black and white cat that resembled a skunk. Each episode of the cartoon utilized the same theme of Pepe chasing the female cat all over Paris, trying to shower her with love and kisses.

At least once every cartoon, Pepe would hold his heart's desire in his arms with her squirming frantically, attempting to break free, because what Pepe didn't realize was that he was a skunk and he stank! As smooth and debonair as Pepe was, he still smelled. In his mind, however, he believed that he was God's gift to the female species. To everyone else that wasn't a skunk, he stank!

When we are practicing sin, I believe that's how we are to the nostrils of God. As former addicts, most of us have wallowed in our mess for a long time. Most of us had to hit rock bottom before we realized that our only way out was up. I had to learn that the only way for me to see my mess was to remove myself from it. I had to stop being a skunk before I could smell my stink. Once I stopped using drugs, I had to separate myself from all drug associations. I had to sanctify myself from any and every thing or body that would contribute to me being a skunk.

When I was younger, people used to ridicule Pentecostals (and some still do) and/or those who were

Holy Sanctified. They were branded as being "Holy Rollers." I'm told that back in the day those were fighting words! I, myself, never really knew what being "sanctified" meant. I learned though to be Holy Sanctified means that you have been set apart for a sacred purpose or religious use, consecrated by God. To me, that is awesome! The fact that God thinks enough about you to choose you and set you apart for an intended sacred purpose!

So now that you have stopped using drugs, you begin to realize that God has a divine purpose for your life, and it is not selling, buying, or using drugs. In order to keep from being enticed and overcome by your past addiction, you have to take the initiative to sanctify or separate yourself from those surroundings. You have to do that to stop being Pepe Le Pew. You must force yourself to smell how bad your stink really is!

Leviticus 11:44 (KJV) says in part that: "For I am the LORD your God: ye shall therefore sanctify yourselves, and ye shall be holy; for I am holy." Leviticus 20:8 (KJV) goes on to say, "And ye shall keep my statutes, and do them: I am the LORD which sanctify you."

You see, when God delivers you, in an instant He also sets you apart. When you accept Christ Jesus in your heart, He washes away all past sins, cleans you as white as snow, and then sanctifies you by setting you apart. In order for you to stay sanctified, you must remove yourself from that unclean thing.

Joshua 3:5 (KJV) says, "Sanctify yourselves: for tomorrow the LORD will do wonders among you." God wants to do wonders among us. He wants to endow us with His Holy Spirit from on high. And after His Spirit has come, we shall receive His power!

Acts 1:8 (KJV) says, "But ye shall receive power, after that the Holy Ghost is come upon you." God wants so many good things for us. He wants us to know that it was He that chose us and not we that have chosen Him. John 15:16 (KJV) says, "Ye have not chosen me, but I have chosen you, and ordained you, that ye should go and bring forth fruit, and that your fruit should remain: that whatsoever ye shall ask of the Father in my name, he may give it you."

So, God has not only chosen us and set us apart, but He has ordained us that we should go out and produce. We can't let the enemy trick us into feelings of worthlessness. God doesn't want us to die from addictions or in bondage. In this era of everyday abortions, if God allowed you to be born, then He has a divine purpose for your life!

I've never been through any drug rehabilitation program. I did go to one Narcotics Anonymous (NA) meeting once after enduring a weekend-long crack binge. I went because it was my first real taste of being sick and tired of my behavior. I never went back, and a few days later I was using again.

I am vaguely familiar with the NA program because my brother successfully went through it and currently has about 14 years clean. He is a dynamic speaker and travels the northern East Coast giving encouragement. What I do know about NA, though, is contrary to my spiritual principles. NA teaches that once an addict always an addict. That may be true for them, but I don't believe it is for believers because that is not what my Holy and wise God told me.

Second Corinthians 5:17 (KJV) says, "Therefore if any man be in Christ, he is a new creature: old things are passed away; behold, all things are become new." *All* things, not *some* things! Once I stood up in church and admitted that I was an addict, the devil had to release those chains of bondage. You see, for too long I didn't believe that I was an addict. I felt that I had control over every aspect of my life. I was in serious denial. I had sat in church through countless testimony services and never opened my mouth. The enemy had me paralyzed with the fear of other people's perceptions of me. I was so concerned with what they might say or think that I entangled my own self with a yoke of bondage!

But, glory to God, when I finally got enough boldness to stand up and voluntarily say that I was a drug addict and the Lord Jesus Christ delivered me, then and only then was I completely free. I immediately felt the anointing of God immerse my body, and a 28-year weight was lifted off my shoulders. I felt as if I'd just snatched the keys to hell from the devil and strolled out of hell, rendering him powerless!

NA also teaches that there are 12 steps to your complete recovery. I don't know about anyone else, but I never took NA's 12 steps. All I took was one step towards Jesus, and Jesus stepped towards me! In an instant, I was delivered from drugs, alcohol, and tobacco, and I no longer care what they say. I'm not concerned with what they say because, first of all, they don't have a heaven or a hell to put me in. They don't know where I've been and what I've been through! And if they would be truthful, they'd admit that they themselves, or someone else in their family, is going through their own hell!

One thing that I will embrace from NA, though, is their maxim of "One day at a time." Not one day at a time because we're so fragile and insecure that we think that if we survived that day without using, then we'll live long enough to try again tomorrow. To the contrary, I embrace it because that is how the Bible instructs us to live our lives for the Lord. To give no thought for the morrow but to be totally dependent upon Him. To have the faith to know that if God allowed you to come to it, then He will certainly see you through it. When you're in Christ and Christ is in you, you have a blessed assurance that no matter how many bombs are dropped, or terrorist attacks succeed, or pitfalls you may endure, you will come out victorious.

One of my favorite Scriptures says that the joy of the Lord is my strength! Knowing and believing that is truly joy, unspeakable joy! Man can't give it, and man certainly can't take it away!

The Lord delivered me from addiction and sanctified me. Once I was sanctified, I realized that I had been a skunk, and I could now smell the stink. Initially, I couldn't worry about all my associates who still smelled. I had to allow the Lord to set me apart and turn me around until He placed my feet on solid ground. But don't think there is anything special about me. Believe me, it is all about Him!

Now I have completely conquered the battle of addiction. And in so doing, I am reaching out now to others who still smell. I am shedding Holy Light on God's plan and desire for all His people to be free from bondage. Instead of being imprisoned, I have become a warrior to be feared by Satan and his empire. God has empowered me to hold the keys from the hell of addiction! I am telling you now not something that I have read but that which I have lived. I have been sanctified, ordained, and equipped by God to keep you from smelling! But don't be confused and believe that I am Superman or some spiritual abnormality. I still occasionally lose a battle on different fronts, but I am striving to be victorious on every hand. Most importantly, I know who I am in Christ, and I have already won the war for my mind.

CHAPTER 5:
AN OFFER THAT YOU CAN'T REFUSE

The more that we diligently seek after God, the more that He will avail and reveal Himself to us. You may be familiar with the term used by people of God that God "called" them into ministry. Many people who have had a calling on their lives will tell you that they didn't always answer their first call.

I believe that if God allowed you to be born, then He definitely has a purpose for your life, no matter who claims that you were illegitimate. When God has called you, it is very difficult to elude or avoid your calling. Because God is omnipresent, wherever you run to, you will run right smack dab into Him. However, a lot of hardheaded types like myself have had to suffer several near-debilitating experiences before we realize that God is trying to get our attention. It takes years for some of us to realize that God has made us an offer that we can no longer refuse.

When we think of 'an offer that we can't refuse', most of us envision an Italian or Sicilian in an Armani pinstriped suit with a name like Lucabrazzi, Gambino, Gotti, or Soprano. But what I want to impress upon you is not about Mario Puzzo's Godfather, but about God, our Heavenly Father. My focus is not on Marlon Brando playing Don Corleone, but it is about the one and only true and living God. What I want to deal with is not about sending someone a smelly bass wrapped in paper signifying that the one they love now eternally sleeps with the fish. No, I want to clarify our inability to escape that which the Lord has called on us to do.

If I were presenting this as a case in a court of law, I would call as a witness a gentleman by the name of Jonah, who found himself sleeping in the belly of a giant fish. Jonah had specific instructions from God to complete a task that God equipped him for. But because of his insecure feelings of fear and rejection, he refused to go to the hood of Nineveh as the Lord had instructed. So, Jonah, like many of us, attempted to flee or escape from that which he was called to do. You see, I, like Jonah, had to learn that when God has called you to do a task, no matter how long and how far you run from Him, you will eventually run right into Him and the destiny that He has ordained for your life.

The point I'm trying to make does not involve someone named Sosa dispatching, from Colombia, a heavily armed hit squad with a life-cancellation contract bearing your name of Scarface on it. I want to tell you how someone named Jehovah can dispatch a heaven-bound prophet with a Holy and precise Word from God to make you an offer that you can't refuse.

If I could call another witness, I would call Jeremiah. As we know, Jeremiah was a major prophet, and his book in the Bible contains important subject matter that dealt with timely messages to God's people of Judah. Jeremiah also issued prophecies concerning the Messiah and the new covenant to come.

The 27th chapter of the book of Jeremiah deals precisely with one of those messages. The Bible tells us that those were trying times for Judah. The nation was caught up in a rapidly changing political whirlwind. You see, although revival and religious reform had followed the finding of the Book of Law during the repair of the temple in 622 BC, the effects of King Josiah's religious beliefs were short-lived. Most of the people of Judah had effectively put God up on a dusty, seldom-used shelf and essentially, in modern terminology, had kicked God to the curb.

False doctrine was abundantly preached by false prophets who told whoever was in power exactly what they wanted to hear. Therefore, God sent a man, a holy messenger, on a spiritual mission to warn His people and make them an offer that they couldn't refuse. So entered Jeremiah, the prophet of God who had grown up and worshipped alongside King Josiah who loved and respected Jeremiah. And now the Lord had sent Jeremiah to extend one final plea to Josiah's son King Jehoiakim for the salvation of Judah—an offer that king couldn't refuse.

He told the king that all you've got to do is make bonds and yokes and place them upon your necks. Tell your peeps in Edom, Moab, Ammon and Sidon to do the same thing. For the Lord has given all these lands unto the hand of Nebuchad-nezzar, the king of Babylon. The Lord said, "If you do these things and serve that king, then you can remain in your land and live your life, and He will sustain you. But if you refuse to heed my true prophet, then woe be unto you, for you will surely die. I will punish you with the sword and dry up your land. Just recognize that I AM that I AM and choose life and not death." (Jeremiah 27)

But how many of us have heard God's precise and Holy Word, yet refused to be a doer of His Word? How many of us have rejected God's offer and pleas to us? How many of us knew that God was telling us to go right but we continued to go left, because it was more comfortable to go left. Or because everyone else was going left and we didn't want to stand alone, or simply because going left, in the fast lane, felt sooo good?

I say unto you, what if Noah had felt that way? Do you think we would still be here today or would God have destroyed the whole Earth, leaving no survivors? The truth of the matter is that if God cannot use you, then He will eventually lose you. He will find someone else to accomplish the task because God's Word cannot return void. So, if He spoke it, then it will come to pass. If you refuse to be the willing vessel that He utilizes, then—believe me—He will find another, and you will forfeit your blessings.

God may desire for you to fulfill a task, but if you're so stiff-necked and rebellious, time after time, then you will fail to see that God is making you an offer that you can't refuse. Believe it or not, most of us would not dare reject an offer from the Godfather or some other infamous gangland character. But when it comes from God our Heavenly Father, too many of us reject His plea or fail to acknowledge that which He is calling us to do.

This is a big mistake. When you attempt to flee from God, you will eventually run right into Him! God may put catastrophic events in your life to get your attention. God has a way of putting you in what I call a "pit experience", where you have no choice but to become dependent upon Him. Hello, somebody.

In John 15:16 (KJV), Jesus makes God's intentions clear. He says: "Ye have not chosen me, but I have chosen you, and ordained you, that ye shall go up and bring forth fruit, and that your fruit should remain; that whatsoever ye shall ask of the Father in my name, he may give it to you." Jesus is making it clear that we didn't choose God, but God has chosen us to do His works, to bear fruit and bear it continually. The best part is that when we do these things, anything that we ask of the Father in Jesus' name will be granted to us!

If we are blessed enough to have God deliver us from drugs, then we must be aware enough to realize that God did not deliver us just so that we could be delivered. If God spared us from the pits of hell's addiction, then He requires us to testify to someone else in bondage and let them know that they, too, can be delivered.

We must offer some mother hope that her child can recover from their nightmare. We must encourage some child that their daddy can get well and be the head of their family once more. We must realize that if God only wanted to deliver us, then He would have delivered us and then allowed us to die. The truth is that God kept us because He loved us and has need of us to go out and win souls for His kingdom.

God could, if He desired, very easily force His will upon us. However, God is a gentleman and a God of choice. He's the leader of a volunteer army. It's not in His nature to force us to do anything. God will equip us to make the right decision when presented with a choice. That's how He operates. He will also sometimes influence our circumstances attempting to get our attention. As in the case of Jonah, who rejected God's instructions, God allowed Him to be swallowed up by a big fish! What that symbolizes is that once God chooses you and you refuse to yield to Him, God will allow your circumstances to overtake you until you come to your spiritual senses. The longer it takes for you to yield, the larger your fish may be. Hello, somebody!

You may find yourself, as I did, in the belly of addiction. You may find yourself, as I did, having a major surgery performed. You may find yourself incarcerated or someplace where everyone else has abandoned you. Oftentimes God will allow you to be separated from everyone and everything else in your life until you come to the realization that your only way out is up—through Him! God will allow you to hit rock bottom, because then and only then is your only way out found by looking up to Him.

In conclusion of this chapter, please note that in our Biblical reference, the king rejected Jeremiah's plea and was therefore overtaken by Nebuchadnezzar and forced out of his kingdom and into bondage. The Lord allowed the people to be enslaved for a period of years before He gracefully overturned their dilemma and allowed them to return to their promised land.

My plea unto you is to not be as hardheaded as I was. I believe that the Lord God Almighty is tugging on someone's heart that's reading this book. I beseech you to yield unto Him. Try Jesus, like I eventually did, after everything else had failed.

The Lord is making you an offer that you cannot refuse. And the reward is life everlasting filled with a peace—oh, what peace! God grants the kind of peace that passes all understanding. ^{Php. 4:7} For me, the peace alone is worth more than I could ever deserve or describe, not having to look over your shoulder for the police or someone you're beefing with, or the brother, boyfriend, or husband of some female you dogged.

I dare you to let go and let God! To do as I did and say as I said, "God, I don't know whether You're real or not. All I know is that I'm sick and tired of being sick and tired, and I don't want to go on living the way I've been living. God, if You are real, then take away the drugs! Take away the addictions! Take away the pain! Lord, save me right now!"

Later that very same night, God put me to the test. He gave me an opportunity to continue in my sin or to be restored. When I remembered my earnest plea and refused to sin, He delivered me that very instant! He delivered me from nearly three decades of drug abuse, alcohol, and tobacco. All three! All in an instant, in the twinkling of an eye!

God is a good God, and He'll keep you only if you want to be kept. Won't you please accept His offer today?

Romans 10:13 (KJV) says, "For whosoever shall call upon the name of the Lord shall be saved." If you have yet to accept Jesus in your life, read this aloud:

> *I believe that Jesus died on the cross for me and that*
> *His blood washed away all my sins. I believe that after*

His death, Jesus rose on the third day with all power in His hands. I believe that Jesus is Lord and Savior and He will come again. Satan, I am no longer yours, and from now and forever more I will serve the Lord Jesus Christ with all my heart, all my mind, and all my soul. Here I am, Lord: send me, I'll go! Here I am, Lord: use me for Your glory.

REDEEMED

CHAPTER 6:
HOW YOU LIVING?

Are you living a good life or a Godly life?

I was going to church on Sundays, and I said my prayers at night. I even tried to live my life by the Golden Rule of "Do unto others as you want them to do unto you." I had a good heart, and I was actually a nice person, if I say so myself. Wasn't I certainly bound for heaven?

I was experiencing a small taste of success in my profession as a computer consultant as well as in my basketball officiating. I had a tiny touch of religion but not much Christianity. In other words, I was not in Christ. I was not a *doer* of God's Word. I was, sadly—like most Christians—a *hearer* only. ^{Jas. 1: 23,25}

Second Timothy 3:5 says that I had a form of godliness but was denying the power thereof. I read that someone once described the contrast between the 'Good Life' and 'A Godly Life' as the difference between the top of the ocean and the bottom of the ocean. On top, sometimes it's like glass: smooth, serene, and calm. Then other times it's raging and stormy. But when you go down hundreds of fathoms below, it's beautiful, consistent, always calm, and always peaceful.

And you see, although I was a good person, living the so-called "good life" of the American Dream, I did not have the peace in my life that only comes from having a personal relationship with Jesus Christ as your Lord and Savior. In fact, there were storms raging in my household, and my marriage was headed for a massive collision with the rocks.

Philippians 4:7 (KJV) says "the peace of God, which passeth all understanding, shall keep your hearts and minds through Christ Jesus." That Scripture is definitely true, but Jesus won't keep that which hasn't been committed to Him, that which hasn't been surrendered to Him, that which hasn't been given completely to Him in faith.

It wasn't until I got in Christ and allowed Christ to get in me that I learned that living the good life and being a good person did not guarantee my salvation. But when you live a Godly life that's rooted in God's Holy Word, you're guaranteed to inherit His promise of eternal life.

John 10:10 (KJV) states, "I [Jesus] have come that they might have life, and that they might have it more abundantly." What Saint John is referring to is the fact that Jesus came not to condemn us but to correct us so that we would come to the full realization of who we are through Him. Once we do that, then we become heirs to the Kingdom of God.

Not everyone will inherit that promise, but only those who have prioritized God as the single most important thing in their lives and not just in lip service. Those who strive to walk daily in the power of the Spirit and not in the flesh. Those whose heart is made perfect towards God and both fear and reverence Him. Those who choose to worship God in both Spirit and in Truth. To make it plain and simple, when you begin living a Godly life, then you automatically inherit the good life!

I had to learn that when you trust and believe and have faith in God, no material possessions, no job, no jewelry, no house, no car, no amount of cash, and no lover are worth the heavenly reward of living a Godly life. Matthew 16:26 asks, "What is a man profited if he shall gain the whole world and lose his own soul?"

In other words, "How you living?" Are you living the good life or a Godly life? Once I woke up to the truth of who I *was* as opposed to who I *am* in Christ, there is no alternative but to live a Godly life. Jesus is the only answer to all our problems today. With all due respect, Allah is not the answer. Buddha is not the answer. Scientific, astrological, and self-inspired ideologies are not the answer. Oprah may have some answers, but she is not *the* answer.

But O! let me tell you about the lover of my soul. His name is Jesus: He who loved me, even before I first loved myself. His name is Jehovah: He who walked this earth for thirty years before He began a ministry that only lasted three years. His name is El Shaddai: He who was born to die, was crucified, and yet rose again on the third day.

BUT WHAT MANNER OF MAN IS THIS?

What manner of man is this who would ask you to give up this one life that you are living that you can see, touch, feel, love, and enjoy? What manner of man is this who would have you give up your precious life—a bird in the hand, so to speak, that you can see, touch, and feel—for a heavenly reward of two birds in the bush, that you can now only imagine?

What manner of man is this who would have you deny all reasonable thinking and rationale? What manner of man is this who would command you to lean not on your own understanding but in all your ways to acknowledge Him? ^{Prov. 3:6}

What manner of man is this who says that he who loves father or mother or son or daughter more than Him is not worthy of Him? ^{Mat. 10:37} What manner of man is this who—after being crucified for a debt that He didn't owe, after paying a price that we couldn't pay—would with His last breath beg His Heavenly Father to forgive those who so savagely slaughtered Him, "for they know not what they do"? [Lk. 23:34]

What manner of man is this who can take drug addicts, prostitutes, adulterers, whoremongers, thieves, millionaires, athletes, murderers, the abandoned and the abused, and have them surrender all to follow Him? What manner of man is this who can take away a lifetime of pain and suffering or a lifetime of sin and shame and throw it into the Sea of Forgetfulness as though it never was?

Many have wondered, *What manner of man is this?* Those who knew Him the best even marveled. Matthew, Mark, Luke, and John all asked, "What manner of man is this that even the winds and the sea obey Him?" (Matthew 8:21, KJV)

I know that some reading this book are still doubters of God's Word. I feel that some who are reading this book are highly educated, financially secure, and able to live any lifestyle that they desire. If I am speaking to you, I only ask you this: *How you living, and do you know Jesus?* Where is your happiness, and would you still have it if you lost all your earthly possessions?

> He that handleth a matter wisely shall find good:
> and whoso trusteth in the LORD, happy is he.
>
> **—Proverbs 16:20 (KJV)**

The tragic events that struck our nation on the 11th of September, 2001 have caused a great deal of people to be emotionally tossed to and fro and looking for answers, but I hear God saying, "Be still and know that I am God!" (Psalm 46:10, KJV) Let me ask you again, "How you living?"

When you are in Christ and living a Godly life, worldly events, no matter how tragic, shouldn't move you. I'm not saying that you shouldn't feel compassion or sorrow. But when you are rooted in your faith, then no circumstances should move you to a point of panic, uncertainty, or despair. For the Word of the Lord in Psalm 55:22 (KJV) says, "Cast thy burden upon the Lord, and he shall sustain thee: he shall never suffer the righteous to be moved."

But what about anthrax?, you may ask. God in His Holy Omnipotence already knew you would have these concerns; that's why He left you His disciple Mark, who wrote in that if they (the disciples of Christ) shall drink any deadly thing, it shall not hurt them. ^{Mk. 16:18}

So, let not your heart be troubled. Simply know that you "can do all things through Christ, which strengtheneth you", and that "God will supply all your need according to His riches in glory by Christ Jesus." [Philippians 4:13,19 (KJV)]

Just give up your good life for His Godly life and you will receive eternal life. "Seek ye first the Kingdom of God, and His righteousness; and all these things shall be added unto you." (Matthew 6:33, KJV) We'll take a closer look at that Scripture in the next chapter, but for now…. *How you living?*

CHAPTER 7:
SEEK YE FIRST

So, now that we are new creatures, no longer desiring to live ignorant to sin but striving to fulfill the will of our Heavenly Father, we may still occasionally find ourselves entangled in our own mess. We can sometimes become so involved with our jobs, our families, and our own agenda that our spiritual growth becomes stagnant. We can and often do justify our 'forever busyness' with the fact that we need some extra money.

We may need extra money for our regular bills, or we may need it for our children's braces or new back-to-school stuff, or maybe a new car or a well-deserved vacation. Regardless of what we need additional money for, we must be careful not to become entangled with additional jobs, constant overtime, or get-rich-quick schemes. When we do become entangled in these and other self-sustaining endeavors, then what we are saying to God is that we don't trust Him to take care of us. What we are ultimately saying is that the Scripture that says that God will supply all our needs is not referring to us. We are, by our actions, implying that we don't embrace those references in Scripture that deal with casting all our cares upon God.

The principle that I'm about to share with you is probably one of the most neglected instructions by Christians today. This is one of the principles that people may say they embrace, but by their sheer deeds they are displaying something contrary. Let's examine the following text.

> [30] Wherefore, if God so clothe the grass in the field, which today is, and tomorrow is cast into the oven, shall he not much more clothe you, O ye of little faith? [31] Therefore take no thought saying, What shall we eat? Or, what shall we drink? Or, Wherewithal, shall we be clothed? [32] (For after all these things do the Gentiles seek:) for your heavenly Father knoweth that ye have need of these things. [33] But seek ye first the Kingdom of God, and his righteousness; and all these things shall be added unto you.
>
> —Matthew 6:30-33 (KJV)

When you're living in God's will, you can have the desires of your heart, if only you seek first the Kingdom of God and His righteousness. From the Sermon on the Mount, Jesus illustrates His point by referring to objects in nature that were immediately at hand. Elsewhere in the Scripture, He uses the birds in the air and the flowers in the field as examples. Jesus asks, "Are we not better than they? Shall He not much more clothe you?" [Matthew 6:30; Luke12:28 (KJV)]

The Bible clearly teaches that God is the Creator and sustainer of nature. Worry and anxiety are known to shorten one's lifespan. So, if God is the Creator and the sustainer, what cause do we have to worry? Somebody once said that if you pray, then you have no business worrying, and if you're worrying, then you have no business praying. What are you worrying for? *O ye of little faith.*

But what *is* faith? Hebrews 11:1 says that faith is the substance of things hoped for, the evidence of things unseen. Quite simply, faith is total confidence in the provision of God. But how can we profess to be true believers, keepers of the flame, redeemers of His promise, inheritors of the throne, sanctified, Holy Ghost-filled, tongue-talking Christians and not possess the faith of one little grain of a mustard seed.

Evidently, we must not possess the faith of a mustard seed because Matthew 17:20 says that if we had it, we could move mountains. When was the last time you spoke to a mountain and moved it? One of the problems may be that all we're doing is speaking *to* it when the word of Matthew 21:22 (KJV) says: "And all things, whatsoever ye shall ask in prayer, believing, ye shall receive."

Uh-oh, there's that P word, PRAYER. Prayer is the fellowship and communication with our Lord—the single most powerful yet most under-utilized weapon of the believer. The one thing that we can always find excuses not to do. I don't know about anyone else, but I'm definitely preaching to myself here.

You see, God dealt with me directly on this. His divine revelation made me realize that like my namesake in the Bible, I am a man of great faith. *But,* I had to ask myself, *is your faith in God? Or is your faith in yourself?*

Before I was saved, I had great confidence in myself. I was a great high school athlete, and like all athletes, I developed and thrived off that confidence. When the going got tough, then the tough got going. And how did we get going? Did we say, "I can do this because I can do all things through Christ Jesus who strengthens me!"? Or did we say, "All right, come on, Steve: you've done it before, you can do this now!"? How many times, as athletes, have we dug deeper into ourselves instead of reaching higher into Him?

How can we *not* have total confidence in the provision of God? How can we *not*, after all that we've read in God's Holy Word? How can we *not*, after all the teaching that we've received and all the preached Word that we've feasted on? How can we *not*, after all the fasting and praying that we've done, after all the tithes and offerings that we've given and sown? How can we *not* have total confidence in the provision of God?

I don't know about you, but I keep finding myself in Matthew 6:33. Are we truly seeking first the Kingdom of God and its righteousness? If we examine closely the context in which Jesus made this statement, you'll find that this was part of the awesome Sermon on the Mount. His disciples, who gave themselves as a living sacrifice, ^{Rom. 12:1} were instructed that they must continue seeking God's Kingdom and its righteousness.

Now, this doesn't mean to go and look for it, then maybe you'll find it and maybe you won't. This instruction was meant to imply a continual or constant seeking of an hourly, a daily, a weekly, a monthly, a yearly, an endless, persistent, committed, and deliberate pursuit of God and His righteousness. We cannot put Him on the shelf while we're in the company of unsaved associates, relatives, teammates, or coaches who use profane language, or engage in sexual promiscuity, or defile their bodies with drugs, alcohol, or tobacco simply because we don't want to be ridiculed and we yearn to be accepted.

Leviticus 10:10 says that there shall be a difference between holy and unholy, clean and unclean.

> But ye are a chosen generation, a royal priesthood, an holy nation, a peculiar people; that ye should shew forth the praises of him who hath called you out of darkness into his marvelous light.
>
> —1 Peter 2: 9 KJV

How can we show forth His praises if we're putting Him on the shelf because we're ashamed of what the world may think! We've got to seek Him as if our lives depended upon it! And guess what? They do! We've got to seek Him and seek Him first. Not as if we're wandering in the desert for forty years, but a deliberate, focused, premeditated, predetermined, and uninterrupted journey to accomplish our Master's will to seek first the Kingdom of God and His righteousness.

We should note that there is an emphasized difference or contrast between the spiritual and the materialistic. We, as Saints of the Most High God, are to seek first the righteousness that is characteristic of God's Kingdom, and then all these things (material and abundant) shall be added unto us. Not during, and certainly not before, but *after* we seek God's Kingdom. Because we have been preapproved for our blessings, God will provide all these things. Prosperity, the houses, the cars, the fat contracts that all but ensure great wealth—all this shall be *added* unto us if we follow God's protocol and only "seek ye first…".

I don't know about you, but I need to be constantly reminded that when our #1 priority is spiritual, then God will take care of all the material things in our lives. You see, sometimes I need to be put in self-check and know that where God guides, He always provides!

I had to learn that we can get so caught up in our daily affairs, our families, our businesses, our sports, our officiating, our hobbies, and even our church work, that we all want to live large and blow up, that we fail to fully mature and grow up, and then we get caught up and won't go up, because in reality we're torn up from the floor up.

David said that he's never "seen the righteous forsaken nor his seed begging for bread." (Psalm 37:25, KJV) If we simply trust in the Lord and have faith that He is able and willing to do everything that He has promised us, then surely it will come to pass. I heard a blessed man of God, the late Bishop David

Wallace of Brooklyn, NY, once say, "If God gives you a task to do and it doesn't face any opposition, then I doubt very seriously that it came from God."

I say that to say this, while you are seeking first the Kingdom of God, be prepared to face tremendous opposition. Especially if you are new in your walk, because the enemy wants to render you useless before you ever come into the complete realization of who you are in Christ and just how powerful you are. The Bible says that one shall chase a thousand and two shall put ten thousand to flight. Deut. 32:30

Another blessed man of God I know teaches that oftentimes the enemy's objective is not to make you do something wrong, but just to keep you from doing what's right. If the enemy can continually keep you from doing what's right, then he can eventually get you to stop going to church, to stop praying, and to stop spreading the Gospel. If the enemy can separate you from the source of your strength, then he can and will eventually destroy you.

My brothers and sisters, despite the opposition in your life, I come to encourage you today that God is more than able—and waiting to grant you—the desires of your heart. Know that no weapon formed against you shall prosper when you're living in the will of God. Isa. 54:17 Endeavor to literally obey Matthew 6:33, seeking first the Kingdom of God and His righteousness, and then all these things shall be added unto you.

CHAPTER 8:

THE PRICE HAS ALREADY BEEN PAID

The Webster's Online Collegiate Dictionary defines the word REDEEMED in the following manner: (1) to buy back: REPUR-CHASE; (2) to free from captivity by payment of ransom, or to free from the consequences of sin; (3) to release from blame or debt; (4) to change for the better: REFORM; (5) to REPAIR, RESTORE.

As a born-again believer, you need to know and understand that your life has been purchased by our Heavenly Father and paid for by the blood of Jesus. But paid to whom, you may wonder? And why was it necessary for anyone to pay anything?

Before God created man, Lucifer was an angel of praise. In fact, he was the most melodious of all the angels. He became so swollen and puffed up on himself, though, by worshipping his gift and not the gift giver, that he convinced himself he should be equal to God. Lucifer started a rebellion in the heavenlies and attempted to persuade any angels that would listen to rebel against God. As punishment, God cast Lucifer and his renegade angels down from heaven and bound them to Earth.

Make no mistake about it, the Earth—this world that we live in—is the domain of Lucifer the fallen angel. For now, he is the ruler of this world. [Jn. 12:31] And because Adam, in his act of disobedience, inadvertently turned the world over to the evil one, Lucifer, *aka* Satan, exercises a certain amount of authority on Earth.

But God, through His infinite wisdom and grace, thwarted Satan's attempt to take over completely. God's plan would be fulfilled even in Adam's failure, because God promised that one day His seed would come through a woman to crush Satan. [Gen. 3:15] Know that God is not a man that He should lie or repent. [Num. 23:19] Know that God's Word cannot come back to Him void. [Isa. 55:11] That means that if God said it, then you can bank on it, for it will come to pass. Pastor Martin Ellerbe once told me that if the wall in your house was the color white and God said that it was the color red, then it would immediately turn red, because God cannot lie!

SPIRITUAL WARFARE

But in the meantime, we are right in the middle of this raging battle, which is known as spiritual warfare. And because we are engaged in this angelic conflict, what we need is spiritual power, which yields the authority to wage victorious warfare.

We need to keep Satan from destroying our families, breaking up our marriages, possessing our children, controlling our minds, and inflaming our passions. We need to evict the devil from our homes, cast him out of our minds, boot him out of our finances, and get him off our backs! We need to put him under our feet!

But where do we get this authority?, you may ask. The most powerful weapon in spiritual warfare is the Word of God. By correctly applying God's Word, you can do what Jesus did and defeat the devil on every term. Studying the Word of God, regular prayer and fasting, and meditating both day and night will inevitably equip the believer for victory in every battle.

I believe that the way we sustain victory in spiritual warfare is to begin exploring the source found in the book of Hebrews, where we discover the answer is a person. In the 2nd chapter of Hebrews, we find that God has sent a person into the spiritual battle and tells us that we need to see this person.

We need to see: Him who was made in man's image, Him who was crowned with glory and honor, Him who was set over the works of God's hands, Him who has all things in subjection under His feet. And who is He? His name is Jesus!

WE NEED TO SEE JESUS!

The same Jesus who by the grace of God should taste death for every man; the same Jesus that sanctifieth, and we who are sanctified by Him become one; the same Jesus who through death might destroy him that had the power of death, that is, the devil; the same Jesus who took not on Him the nature of angels but who took on Him the seed of Abraham, thus fulfilling God's promise that His seed was come through a woman to destroy the devil.

If we're going to be winners in spiritual battle day in and day out, week after week, time and time again, we need to see Jesus. The key to having authority in spiritual warfare is to "see Jesus"—to understand and put into practice all that He has purchased for us by His death; to exercise the authority that we received through His resurrection; and to fulfill the dominion that we inherited through His ascension.

If we could only see Jesus, we would see not just someone, but our Savior, who has already won the battle for us. It is our inability to see Jesus that has limited our authority in the realm of the angelic conflict and spiritual warfare. When we can see Jesus in this context, we will be introduced to authority we never knew possible.

Once you begin to see Jesus, then you will begin to embrace Him as your redeemer. Remember, to be redeemed means that you were bought back, that you were repurchased to be rescued from captivity by payment of a ransom, and that you have been extricated from trouble or sin. You see, the price has already been paid.

Too many times, our enemy who was labeled as "the accuser of our brethren" [Rev. 12:10] uses our sins and faults to attempt to spiritually blackmail us into believing that we're not worthy to praise God. The devil attempts to deceive us into thinking that we must be burdened down with guilt and shame. However, the Bible tells us that "all have , sinned and come short of the glory of God". (Romans 3:23, KJV) and that "there is therefore now no condemnation to them which are in Christ Jesus." (Romans 8:1, KJV)

BUT WHO IS IN CHRIST JESUS?

We who have proclaimed Him Lord and Savior believe that He died for us yet rose again. We, the chosen, believe that there is no other way to the Father but by Him, the Son. And once you know that you are in Christ Jesus and that He lives in you, you become a joint heir to our Father's riches and glory, and no devil in hell can keep you from your heavenly inheritance.

Galatians 4:4-7 (KJV) says:

> [4] But when the fulness of the time was come, God sent forth his Son, made of a woman, made under the law, [5] To redeem them that were under the law, that we might receive the adoption of sons. [6] And because ye are sons, God hath sent forth the Spirit of his Son into your hearts, crying, Abba, Father. [7] Wherefore thou art no more a servant, but a son; and if a son, then an heir of God through Christ.

Jesus was born of a woman, which means He was human. He was born as a Jew, which means He was subject to God's Law and fulfilled it perfectly. Thus Jesus was the perfect sacrifice because, although He was fully human, He never sinned. He was the ultimate sacrifice. Jesus was the only one capable of paying such a massive debt. His death bought freedom for all in the world who were enslaved to sin so that we could be adopted into His family. Hallelujah!

Under Roman law, the adopted child was guaranteed all legal rights to his father's property. He was not a second-class son; he was equal to any other sons, biological or adopted, in his father's family. As adopted children of God, we share with Jesus His inheritance and all the rights to God's resources. As God's heirs, we can claim what He has already provided for us. We are the righteousness of God. We were chosen to share in His royalty.

First Peter 2:9 (KJV) tells us: "But ye are a chosen generation, a royal priesthood, an holy nation, a peculiar people; that ye should shew forth the praises of him who hath called you out of darkness into his marvellous light." All we have to do is show Him praise. Praise Him in the face of our enemy! Shame the devil by praising God in the midst of our mess! If you do that, God will turn your mess into a miracle!

Yes, you lost your job, but you should shout out, "Praise God!" Yes, you're misunderstood and being treated unfairly, but, in spite of your situation, shout out, "Praise God!" Yes, your spouse is being tricked by the enemy and there is trouble on every hand, but shout out, "Praise God!" Yes, your child is in jail or has been shot or has murdered someone else, but we've got to learn how to continuously shout out, "Praise God!"

Why say, "Praise God" in situations like this, you may wonder? Because if it hadn't been for God's grace and mercy, our situation could always be worse! Hello, somebody! Despite our situation, in spite of what we're going through, in spite of what we feel, we've got to continually praise our God! Once you understand and believe that the price has already been paid—and knowing that Christ did not come to condemn us but to correct us and that He has already made us joint heirs to His heavenly throne [Rom. 8:17]—how can we not praise Him?

The Bible says to let everything that has breath praise the Lord! If we don't praise God, then the rocks will cry out! [Lk. 19:40] I don't know about you, but I don't want no rocks crying out for me! We are free from sin because Jesus has already paid the price! He has led us out of darkness and into His marvellous light! 1 [Pet. 2:9] Praise God!

There is no need to beat yourself up for what you did or didn't do in your past. I don't care how smart, wonderful, and gifted you are, you cannot change one thing that happened, even as recent as one second ago. You may have fallen; so what? Get up! You may be on the wrong path; so what? Turn yourself around! You may have rejected God; so what? Repent and embrace Him now as if your life depends on it!

Realize that even if you have walked away from God, or if you are still lost and have yet to accept Him as your Lord and Savior, stop right now and repeat this prayer:

> *I believe that Jesus Christ is Lord and Savior. I believe in my heart that Jesus died on the cross for my sins and that You, Father God, raised Him from the dead. I believe that the devil's hold on me has from this moment forward been forever broken. I believe that greater is God that is in me than he that is in the world. I believe that God has just forgiven me for all my sins thanks to Jesus Christ, the lover, and the Redeemer of my soul.*

Now tell the Lord thank you for another chance. Bow down before Him, or jump up and down, or run in place! Although you may have just been saved, never forget that over two thousand years ago, the price had already been paid.

CHAPTER 9:
WHEN THE BITTER BECOMES THE SWEET

The Word of God tells us that as believers we will be faced with trials and tribulations. When we are redeemed by the blood of Christ, we will suffer for His name's sake. As God continues to purge us and make us as pure gold, we will find ourselves having to overcome many obstacles.

The more that we grow in Christ, the more we understand that we are called to endure until the very end, ^{Mat. 24:13} and believe me, it's not over until God says it's over. Therefore, we must realize that failure is not a bad thing, but quitting is. As long as we hang in there and hold on to our faith, God will eventually bring us out of every dilemma.

I would be lying to you if I told you that I never thought about giving up. There are times that the attack of the enemy seems so sustained and intense that you feel like Marvin Gaye when he said that it makes you wanna holla and throw up both your hands! But you know what? No matter how difficult things seem, they could always be worse. If you don't believe me, just read the book of Job.

Job endured his afflictions for decades, and when he eventually came out of his dilemma, God rewarded him with double for his trouble. There is, however, a point where God can take what the enemy meant for your harm and flip the script and turn it into something for your good. There is a point where God can take your bitter situation and turn it into something sweet.

Most of you reading this don't know me and may have difficulty taking my word for anything I say, so allow me to take you on a Biblical journey. Venture with me through the wilderness outside of Egypt and see if you can identify with or find yourself in this re-creation.

> [22] So Moses brought Israel from the Red sea, and they went out into the wilderness of Shur; and they went three days in the wilderness, and found no water. [23] And when they came to Marah, they could not drink of the waters of Marah, for they were bitter: therefore the name of it was called Marah. [24] And the people murmured against Moses, saying, What shall we drink? [25] And he cried unto the LORD; and the LORD shewed him a tree, which when he had cast into the waters, the waters were made sweet: there he made for them a statute and an ordinance, and there he proved them, [26] And said, If thou wilt diligently hearken to the voice of the LORD thy God, and wilt do that which is right in his sight, and wilt give ear to his commandments, and keep all his statutes, I will put none of these diseases upon thee, which I have brought upon the Egyptians: for I am the LORD that healeth thee.

> **—Exodus 15:22-26 (KJV)**

This story unfolds as the Israelites are being led out of captivity in search of the Promised Land. The Bible says that they had been in the wilderness for three days and they had no water to drink. If you were to research this further, you'd find that they had traveled an estimated eleven miles each day, which meant that they'd gone thirty-three miles without water. Imagine that, thirty-three miles in the wilderness without so much as a drop of water to wet their whistle.

Then, suddenly, they come upon a place where there was a body of water. But the place is named Marah, which means 'bitterness', and the water was bitter and could not be consumed. So, what did the people do? They verbally attacked Moses, crying out like babies. Saying, "What are we to drink?" and "We ought to go back to Egypt."

Now understand, it was only three days ago that these same, ungrateful Janet-Jackson-what-have-you-done-for-me-lately people had just experienced what was arguably one of the greatest displays of God's awesome power. This happened when God parted the Red Sea, long enough for these same complaining Israelites to pass, and then God let the sea close on the pursuing Egyptians.

It was only three days ago when Moses said to these people: "Fear ye not, stand still, and see the salvation of the LORD, which he will shew to you today: for the Egyptians whom ye have seen today, ye shall see them again no more for ever. The LORD shall fight for you, and ye shall hold your peace." (Exodus 14:13-14, KJV)

Now, three days later, these people were once again in a place of doubt. So, Moses cried unto the Lord, and the Lord showed him a tree and instructed him to throw that tree into the body of water, and when Moses harkened unto the voice of the Lord and did what he was instructed to do, instantly the bitter became sweet!

Have you ever been in a state of wilderness and it seems like you just can't come out? You've been walking in the wilderness for a matter of days and with nothing to drink. You've been unemployed for too long! You've been broke for too long! You've been struggling with the same issue or issues for too long!

And then, suddenly, you come upon what appears to be what you've been looking for, oh, so long. You finally get a man or you finally find a woman. They look real good and they smell even better. They talk a mighty good game. But when you get to really know them, you find out that their spiritual name is Marah and they're filled with bitterness. And then you begin to grumble and complain, and instead of crying out to God, you begin to doubt your God.

You forget all about last week, when God delivered you from your enemy. You forget all about the bills that you couldn't pay but God made a way. You forget all about how He protected your children, when after you corrected them, they stormed out of the house and you didn't see them all day. You forget all about how He's kept you in your right mind when others, all around you, were losing theirs. You forget all about how He healed your body when sickness and death was all around you. You forget all about how the enemy was raging like a flash flood and it seemed like there was no defense and God provided a way for your escape.

But I hear the voice of Moses saying, *"Be encouraged, my brother, and don't be dismayed. If thou shalt diligently harken to the voice of the Lord thy God, and wilt do that which is right in His sight, and wilt give ear to His commandments, and keep all His statutes, I will put none of these diseases upon thee, which I have brought upon the Egyptians, for I am the Lord that healeth thee."*

So, go now, my brother, and pick up that tree. Carry on, my sister, and take all your burdens and cast them into the water that you desire to drink. Let go and let God. That's when the bitter will become the sweet! That's when God will give you the desires of your heart. Don't grumble and complain, but be obedient unto the Word of God.

Remember the words of our brother Peter, who said, "Humble yourselves therefore under the mighty hand of God, that he may exalt you in due time: Casting all your care upon him; for he careth for you." (1 Peter 5:6-7, KJV)

But you may say, "Brother preacher, that all sounds real, real good. But sometimes, I need a word to restore my joy. I need a word that will strengthen my spirit. I need a word that assures me that everything will be all right."

And what I say to you then is, fret not, my brother, and worry not, my sister, for the joy of the Lord is our strength. [Neh. 8:10] I'll say to you, just take a stroll with me through the Hebrews Hall of Faith. Study the 11th chapter of Hebrews, and you'll see a testament to those of great faith.

Know, my brother and my sister, that if you want the bitter to become the sweet, you've got to have faith in God. You need "genuine faith" that perseveres till the end. Know that emotional decisions rarely last. True faith continues to believe in the truth, even when it seems like you've been denied time and time again.

Know that there is superiority in God's new covenant with us. The last verse in the 11th chapter of Hebrews says that, "God having provided some better thing for us, that they without us should not be made perfect." (Hebrews 11:40, KJV)

Know that God saved this "better thing"—the fulfillment of His promise for us. But in order for us to receive His promise today, we must continue to adhere to and obey His commandments of yesterday. We must be doers of the Word, and not hearers only. [Jas. 1:22]

We must continue to stand still and see the salvation of the Lord! [Exo. 14:13] We must know and believe that no weapon formed against us shall prosper! [Isa. 54:17] We must know that whatever fails to destroy us will ultimately make us stronger! We must keep God's commandments and always do those things that are pleasing to Him. [Jn. 8:29] We must be obedient, my friend, for Samuel said to obey is better than sacrifice! [1 Sam. 15:22]

That's when the bitter will become the sweet! That's when God will uphold His Word! That's when His promises are yours for the asking! Oh, taste and see that the Lord is good! Ps. 43:8 His mercy endureth forever! And He is surely sweeter as the days go by. Be neither discouraged nor dismayed, for our Lord Jehovah will never leave us nor forsake us, and every promise in the Bible is true.

PART 3:

RESTORED

CHAPTER 10:
CHECK YOURSELF SO YOU CAN CORRECT YOURSELF

As a little boy, my paternal grandmother religiously took my brother and me to church. However, when my parents divorced and my mother, brother and I moved away, going to church was not on our agenda. Therefore, when I was born again and began to live a Godly life, the Bible illuminated many dark areas of my life and my character.

Invariably, subconsciously I began to condemn myself for sins that I previously committed or commandments I neglected to fulfill. God's Holy Spirit eventually had to confront me and make me understand that Jesus came into this world not to condemn the world, but through Jesus the world might be saved. In other words, Jesus came to correct us.

Correction, however, is not always an easy task. Many adults find it difficult to accept criticism from loved ones, pastors, teachers, and even God. Men, in particular, often reject correction from anyone. I believe that if we can continually self-check, we can begin to correct ourselves, and then we won't be so quick to condemn ourselves. Romans 8:1 (KJV) says: "There is therefore now no condemnation to them which are in Christ Jesus, who walk not after the flesh, but after the Spirit."

After some extensive Bible study, I received revelation for this chapter from First Chronicles, which was written approximately 430 BC. Ezra is credited with being the author of this Old Testament book which records events occurring between a forty-year span from 1000 BC to 960 BC. First Chronicles parallels Second Samuel and serves as additional commentary to it, even often complementing it. First and Second Chronicles follow Second Kings, which ends with both Israel and Judah in captivity. Written after that captivity, Chronicles summarizes Israel's history, specifically emphasizing the Jewish people's spiritual heritage in an attempt to unify the nation.

Ezra is selective in his telling of this portion of history. The Northern Kingdom is virtually ignored, and in the Southern Kingdom, David's triumphs—not his sins—are recalled. and the Temple is given great prominence as the vital center of national life. The Temple, which was the "church" of that era, was the Mecca or hub of all daily activity. It was the lifeline of the community.

Chronicles begins with Adam, and for the first nine chapters it gives us a "Who's Who" of Israel's history with special emphasis on David's royal line. First Chronicles is a strong reminder of the necessity for tracing our holy roots, thus rediscovering our proven foundation. You see, we need to know our Godly heritage. We need to thank God for our spiritual forefathers. We need to thank God for those spiritual patriots who stood on the principles of Holiness. And we need to recommit ourselves to our passing on of God's uncompromising truth to the next generation, which is, inescapably, our future.

With that background in mind, the Lord has led me to this chapter title for our edification, "Check Yourself So You Can Correct Yourself." This chapter closely follows the WORD so you may want to follow along in your Bible. Let's begin at First Chronicles 9:1-3...

> [1] So all Israel were reckoned by genealogies; and, behold, they were written in the book of the kings of Israel and Judah, who were carried away to Babylon for their transgression. [2] Now the first inhabitants that dwelt in their possessions in their cities were, the Israelites, the priests, Levites, and the Nethinims. [3] And in Jerusalem dwelt of the children of Judah, and of the children of Benjamin, and of the children of Ephraim, and Manasseh.

—1 Chronicles 9:1–3

The transgression or sin of God's people was idolatry, which we know is the worshipping of idols or other Gods. Although every person in Judah did not worship idols, the entire nation was carried away into captivity. Everyone was affected by the sin of some. You see, even if we don't participate in a certain widespread wrongdoing, we will still be affected by those who do. It is not enough to say, "I don't do it." We still need to speak out against the sins of our society.

I believe that it is that very fact that makes Christians who are opposed to abortion, so adamant and vigilant in their means to abolish it. What some extremists fail to realize though is that God does not need us to execute His supreme judgment for Him. I believe that God can and will handle His business, regarding abortion and everything else, at His appropriate time and as He sees fit. In addition to voicing our moral opposition as Christians, what we can do is continue to protest and lobby and vote for those politicians who answer to our same higher calling.

Somebody needs to tell the young people that you cannot hang around with people that you know are doing wrong and committing sin. Even if you are not participating in what they do, if you are present and are not speaking out against their wrongdoing, then I believe that God will see you as guilty by association. And even if you do tell them that what they are doing is wrong, and they continue to do wrong, then you need to get away from them. Sanctify yourself by separating yourself. Check yourself so you can correct yourself.

First Chronicles 9:2 reveals that only two of the original twelve tribes of Israel returned from exile: the tribes of Judah and the tribes of Benjamin.

WE NEED TO RE-EVALUATE OUR WORSHIP!

The Priests and the Levites, according to Exodus the 28th chapter, originated at a time when God was teaching His people how to worship Him. I believe that the Lord is telling us that, once again, He needs to teach us how to worship Him. You see, we can't just worship God any ol' way. 1We can't just offer up any kind of praise. We have to literally worship Him in spirit and in truth. [Jn. 4:23-24]

We have to worship Him for the awesome God that He is. Worship has to become just as important in our services as any other portion, including the preached word. It is during worship that we can tell God just how much we love and adore Him. It is during worship that we can show and tell God just how grateful we are to have a relationship with Him. And it is during worship that God will move on our behalf.

We have to worship Him by giving our best sacrifice of praise! [Jer. 33:11; Heb. 13:15] And we can't give God our best praise if we are not daily consecrating ourselves before, during, and after our worship. We cannot be outside the church socializing during the prayer service and then run down front and instantly lead the congregation in worship.

We cannot lead the congregation in worship and then go right to chewing gum, passing candy and notes, and talking while the preachers of God's Holy Word are in the pulpit. We must be careful of how we conduct ourselves before, during, and after we worship. We must remain both prayerful and watchful. I offer this not to condemn but to amplify or draw attention to this topic so that you may check yourself and can then correct yourself.

The Nethinims were the Temple servants who were responsible for the preparation of worship and the daily administration of the Temple. It is no coincidence that Ezra mentioned them in the same context with the priests and the Levites. In truth, if you hold any position in the church, then you are a servant. God has called you into servanthood. He has called you to humble yourself and serve. If you think that God has called you so that you can be seen in the pulpit, or heard on the radio, or acknowledged at the convocation, then you need to mortify your flesh and check yourself, so that you can correct yourself.

Still, when we think of doing God's work, usually preaching, teaching, singing, and other kinds of visible, up-front leadership come to mind. But know this: whatever role you have in God's Church, it is an important role to God. God greatly appreciates your service, but more importantly, He appreciates that you have the right attitude while serving. In fact, He wants your attitude to be so Spirit-led that it becomes contagious. When you reflect the right attitude, it should reproduce itself in others around you. It should begin to bear fruit. So, where is our fruit?

First Chronicles 9:17-18 gives recognition to the porters—the gatekeepers. They guarded the four main entrances to the Temple and opened the gates each morning for those who wanted to worship. This was not only a privilege, it was a birthright! Uh-oh, God is dealing directly now with the deacons and ministers and everybody else with keys to the church. How many times have we griped or complained and neglected our responsibility when it comes to opening the doors or locking up God's temple?

You can be a deacon for over twenty years, but if every time you have to open or close the church you moan and complain, then I don't believe that God can get any glory out of your service. Now, the younger deacons should look out for the older ones and not make them have to continually do tasks that they can relieve them of. Remember that one day, if it's in God's will, we may be in the same position. Let's check ourselves so we can correct ourselves.

In addition to being gatekeepers, the porters also did other day-to-day chores to keep the Temple running smoothly. This included cleaning the various rooms of the Temple. It included preparing the offerings for sacrifice, and accounting for the gifts designated to the Temple. And again, this was a birthright, a holy and divine privilege; not just anyone could be appointed to these tasks.

Those who appointed the porters needed to know that not only did they fear God and were upright individuals, but they also wanted to know, who's your daddy? Who was your mamma? What seed produced you? Were you good fruit? Because they strongly believed that one bad apple could spoil the whole barrel, and this was too sacred a job to risk having a bad seed. That same premise has carried over into many ministries, and that's why today, a lot of pastors insist that you need to be Holy Ghost-filled to hold any servanthood position in the church.

Gatekeepers had to be reliable, honest, and trustworthy. The people in our churches who handle the offerings and care for the materials and functions of the building follow in a great tradition, and when they are reliable, we should honor them for their service. Even though their ultimate reward is heaven and their record is on high, we—God's chosen people whom they are serving—should not take their commitment for granted. The Bible says to give honor where honor is due. When is the last time we honored these individuals with something other than, by the way, lip service?

Many of us are quick to criticize when a gatekeeper is late or they urge us to leave the building in a timely manner. But when is the last time that you were at your church before 5:30 a.m. to open up for prayer? When was the last time that you volunteered to stay and help them secure the house of the Lord? We need to check ourselves so we can correct ourselves.

Let's revisit the Word.

> [25] And their brethren, which were in their villages, were to come after seven days from time to time with them. [26] For these Levites, the four chief porters, were in their set office, and were over the chambers and treasuries of the house of God. [27] And they lodged round about the house of God, because the charge was upon them, and the opening thereof every morning pertained to them. [28] And certain of them had the charge of the ministering vessels, that they should bring them in and out by tale. [29] Some of them also were appointed to oversee the vessels, and all the instruments of the sanctuary, and the fine flour, and the wine, and the oil, and the frankincense, and the spices. [30] And some of the sons of the priests made the ointment of the spices. [31] And Mattithiah, one of the Levites, who was the firstborn of Shallum the Korahite, had the set office over the things that were made in the pans. [32] And other of their brethren, of the sons of the Kohathites, were over the shewbread, to prepare it every sabbath. [33] And these are the singers, chief of the fathers of the Levites, who remaining in the chambers were free: for they were employed in that work day and night. [34] These chief fathers of the Levites were chief throughout their generations; these dwelt at Jerusalem.

> —1 Chronicles 9:25-34 (KJV)

The Word shows that the Levites oversaw virtually all aspects of the Temple. They were the gatekeepers, the preachers, the teachers, and the singers. They were in charge of worshipping God. They were entrusted with this authority because they were faithful people. Most of us don't know that because of the sins of Levi, his descendants the Levites were not listed as one of the original twelve tribes of Israel. But say to yourself, "just remain faithful."

For even though the Levites were not credited with being one of the original twelve tribes of Israel, they didn't mumble and grumble and complain. And when the other tribes began to engage in idolatry and worshipped false Gods, the Levites refused, and God rewarded them for being faithful. God knew that He could trust them. He knew that they weren't ready, but because they were faithful, if He just showed them how to worship, then He could place them in charge.

If that is your desire, does God know that He can trust you to be in charge of leading others to worship Him? Once again, people, God is saying that we need to again learn how to worship Him. God has granted us another opportunity today to check ourselves so that we can correct ourselves. And if you're reading this book today and you're honest with yourself and you want God to know that He can trust you, for servanthood, then you need to surrender your heart for His service. Pray this prayer, aloud:

> *Heavenly Father, hallowed be Thy name. We surrender our hearts for Your service on this day and forevermore. We ask You, dear God, to create in us a clean heart and renew the right spirit within us.* Ps. 51:10 *Father, fight against that which is fighting against us. Whatever it is that is hindering us, Father, purge it and remove it right now. Father, we pray that You forgive us for our past transgressions and prepare us for our future service.*

Father God, in the name of Jesus, meet us and anoint us where we are so that we can check ourselves so that we may correct ourselves. And when You do this, Father, we will be so careful to give You all the praise and all the glory that You and You alone deserve. Thank You, Lord. Amen.

CHAPTER 11:
TAKE THE PLUNGE!

As a member of the modern day Church of the 21st century, I believe that we, the Church, are what's wrong with the world, and not the other way around. In most metropolitan areas, there are churches on every other corner and in every other block, yet the masses remain enslaved by the trickery and wiles of the enemy.

If Christians are still living in bondage, then no wonder our communities are in decay. Are we no longer our brother's keeper? Are we living in a season where we look only after our own and leave those around us, who are different or who have yet to embrace the light, to fend for themselves?

Didn't Jesus command us to go out unto all the land and preach the Gospel? Are we not required by God to win souls for His kingdom? Well, let me put it this way: if God only wanted us to be saved to experience and enjoy our own personal salvation, then we might as well get saved and then go straight to heaven. Aren't we called to testify to His goodness to help someone else overcome? I believe so, and that it my driving motivation for this book.

But what has happened to us? Mega-ministries are springing up all over the nation, and it appears that churches are more concerned with their seating capacity than they are with their sending capacity. It appears that more and more preachers are more concerned with preaching only prosperity than they are with preaching the Gospel of Jesus. It appears that more and more Christians are becoming spiritual gypsies and have no problem with having their names on numerous church rosters. Then, they don't hesitate to abandon ministries when rebuked by the pastor or offended by the slightest occurrence or ill-placed word.

Something is wrong when TV Evangelists have more influence over you than the Word of God. Something is misplaced when we neglect to assemble ourselves and feel that watching Bobby Jones' Gospel on Sunday morning is sufficient or equivalent to attending church that day. Something is wrong when we think it a crime to give $20 in a normal church offering but won't hesitate to give $200 when the traveling evangelist prophesies us homes, cars, or a long-awaited spouse.

But how and why are we in this mess? What are we not doing? Has God changed His requirements because society is much more liberal and tolerant of others? Because devil worshippers have a right to practice their disbeliefs, does it mean that there is no place for prayer in schools? Why and how long will the church stand idle while our nation promotes sin as an acceptable standard of living?

As in Biblical times past, we are living in a time of trouble, a day of blasphemy and a season of rebuke. The Church is in serious trouble. I believe the Church is in serious trouble because there are thousands of so-called Christians who are embracing the religion of Christ but denying the power thereof. [2 Tim. 3:5] There are countless Christians who feel that as long as they treat people nice, go to church on most Sundays, and don't commit any crimes against society, they don't need holiness to go to heaven.

There are many more Christians who will tell you that tarrying for the Holy Ghost was a thing of the past. They will tell you that one can be taught to speak in other tongues, without the power of the Holy Ghost coming upon them. They will tell you that you don't need to fast to get closer to God. I even had one Christian brother tell me that paying tithes is not a Biblical principle but a personal choice. And after I thought about it, I told him, you're absolutely right, and so is going to hell! God doesn't send you, but you make a personal choice to go.

There are some Christians who have been in church all their lives, yet they have become stagnant and complacent in their faith. They are hesitant to embrace those who are coming into the Kingdom of God, thirsting after righteousness, and seeking the face of God. I believe that God's mandate for us certainly has not changed, but what has changed are the methods in which God is spreading His Gospel.

I've heard other so-called Christians say that there's nothing wrong with having a glass of wine with their dinner for they drank wine in the Bible. You'll hear Christians say that there's no need to be in church three times a week. Time and time again, you'll hear Christians say that it doesn't take all that stuff that those strange Pentecostal, Charismatic, Apostolic, and COGIC people do.

Well, brothers and sisters of the kingdom, I beg to differ. My Bible tells me that it takes all that and some. And any time that you spend in the presence of God is time that you'll never live long enough to regret! With that in mind, I beseech you today to cast off the shackles of mediocrity and "Take the Plunge!"

You see, we serve a mighty God! One who is omnipresent, and I believe He has called us not to be Pentecostals, but He has called us to live holy! In addition to our never-ending pursuit of holiness, we must diligently seek to establish and nurture our personal relationship with Him! Reminiscent of that old Nestea commercial—you might remember, the one when they used to say, "Take the Nestea plunge!"

To better receive what I am attempting to share with you, you should examine the entire epistle of First Peter. The Lord led me to First Peter because it, too, was written in a time of trouble, a day of blasphemy, and a season of rebuke. Christians were being persecuted not only in Rome but also throughout Nero's empire.

Peter wrote this epistle to God's people scattered throughout what is now known as northern Asia because he already knew, around the year 65 A.D., what the Christians' destiny was. He knew and understood that the Christians' destiny was salvation. In order for salvation to take place, I believe you've got to "Take the Plunge."

First Peter 1:13-25 deals with the products of salvation:

> [13] Wherefore gird up the loins of your mind, be sober, and hope to the end for the grace that is to be brought unto you at the revelation of Jesus Christ; [14[As obedient children, not fashioning yourselves according to the former lusts in your ignorance: [15[But as he which hath called you is holy, so be ye holy in all manner of conversation; [16] Because it is written, Be ye holy; for I am holy. [17] And if ye call on the Father, who without respect of persons judgeth according to every man's work, pass the time of your sojourning here in fear: [18] Forasmuch as ye know that ye were not redeemed with corruptible things, as silver and gold, from your vain conversation received by tradition from your fathers; [19] But with the precious blood of Christ, as of a lamb without blemish and without spot: [20] Who verily was foreordained before the foundation of the world, but was manifest in these last times for you, [21] Who by him do believe in God, that raised him up from the dead, and gave him glory; that your faith and hope might be in God. [22] Seeing ye have purified your souls in obeying the truth through the Spirit

unto unfeigned love of the brethren, see that ye love one another with a pure heart fervently: [23] Being born again, not of corruptible seed, but of incorruptible, by the word of God, which liveth and abideth for ever. [24] For all flesh is as grass, and all the glory of man as the flower of grass. The grass withereth, and the flower thereof falleth away: [25] But the word of the Lord endureth for ever. And this is the word which by the gospel is preached unto you.

—1 Peter 1:13-25 (KJV)

The products of salvation are hope, holiness, reverence, and love. Allow me to use as an analogy from that same Nestea commercial, when people would take a glass of Nestea and dive, fully clothed, into a pool of water. Now they didn't just stick their toes in to test the water, but when they took the Nestea Plunge, nobody had to tell you, but you knew beyond a shadow of a doubt that when they came out of that pool, they were going to be what? Wet!

Well, it's the same way with God! When you take the plunge and are immersed in the Holy Spirit... Good God from Zion! When you come up you, too, will be covered with something that everybody can see. You won't be covered with water, but you'll be covered in grace, you'll be saturated in holiness, you'll be drenched in faith, and you'll be dripping with love! Don't just stick your toes in; just take the plunge!

In my spirit I can see and hear Satan in some of your ears telling you that you know it doesn't take all that. Well, right about now, you should be fed up enough to slap Satan right upside his head. You should be fed up enough to cast the devil out of your mind, out of your home, and out of your life! We've got the authority to do it!

Satan is a defeated foe! He's a toothless lion seeking whom he may devour. [1 Pet. 5:8] Resist his temptation, and he will flee from you. [Jas. 4:7] We are made victorious not by our power or by our might, but through Christ Jesus we are more than conquerors! [Rom. 8:37]

If you truly take the plunge, then you're coming up with power from on high. You're coming up equipped for spiritual warfare. You're coming up created with a clean heart and renewed with the right spirit within. [Ps. 51:10] You're coming up victorious!

Satan doesn't want you to realize what it takes to proclaim and sustain your victory! Satan wants you to remain powerless in the spirit. Satan wants you to be so consumed with the world and your flesh that your logical, systematic, scientific, and highly educated thought processes will never allow you to embrace the simple truth of who you are in Christ Jesus and why you have to take the plunge into holiness.

The late District Missionary Lucille Miles often preached a message entitled "Holiness or Hell." And once you heard that message from this Holy Ghost-filled, power-packing woman of God, your walk with God will never be the same. She made it plain by crying loud and sparing not!

So, I encourage you today to look past the conventional reasoning of doctrinal religion and denominational barriers and realize that our salvation is dependent upon our individual relationship with God. Know that our relationship with God must first be established through His Son, Jesus Christ.

Too many people today are claiming to know God but are omitting Jesus. Too many folks today claim to be spiritual but embrace not God's Holy Spirit. My Bible tells me that no man comes to the Heavenly Father, but by the glorious Son. [Jn. 14:6] I stand before you today as a living testimony that there is power in the name of Jesus! We are endued with His Holy power from on high, [Lk. 24:49] but unless we choose to use it, it won't do us any good. So, take the plunge!

God has no need for lukewarm saints. We need to spend much less time busying ourselves with the business of church and be more about our Heavenly Father's business. Regardless of what your title is or whether or not you even have a title, we need to renew our press to bring lost souls into the Kingdom.

Don't worry about what they look like or what they smell like. Concern yourselves not with what their sin or story is. Just know and believe that after we take the plunge, then the Holy Trinity will equip us to practice wisdom and bring them in. It's not up to us to save them, it's only up to us to bring them in. And once they come in, don't be so insecure to worry about what God is using them to do. If you purpose in your heart to take the plunge, then God certainly will use you also.

CHAPTER 12:
SPIRITUAL CPR

Just as individual Christians need to take the plunge and not be lukewarm saints, the church body needs to be revived. In this the year of our Lord, the Church needs CPR. Just as CPR is used in the world to resuscitate a dying body, today's Church needs a spiritual resuscitation.

"But the church is not dying", you may say. Mega-churches with thousands of members are sprouting up every day. Nationally and across the globe, more and more people are becoming awakened to spirituality. Crosses, some bearing the likeness of Jesus, are the number one selling charm in jewelry stores in every major city. In fact, you might say that religion today is very much in vogue.

So, with all this transpiring, one may ask, *How is the Church dying?* I believe the Church is dying because there are very few signs and wonders trailing us. Where are the fruits of a healthy and growing vessel?

There are many believers with varying degrees of faith, but where are the works? My Bible says in James 2:20 (KJV) that "faith without works is dead." And in James 2:26 (KJV), it goes on to say, "For as the body without the spirit is dead, so faith without works is dead also."

So, if there are no works, if there are no signs and wonders, if there are no fruits, then I repeat that the church needs CPR! We need a holy resuscitation to raise us out of the belly of mediocrity. We need to be spiritually shocked out of our comfortable dwelling place in yesterday's anointing. We need to be revived by having our gifts stirred up, our spirits shook up, and our souls set on fire!

To perform spiritual resuscitation, the church needs spiritual CPR. The spiritual CPR that we need means to be more:

Consistent

Persistent

and Resistant

CONSISTENCY

Today's church, the body of Christ, assembled baptized believers' needs to be more consistent. We must develop consistency to continually renew our relationship with God. Grandmomma's anointing just won't do. We must be consistent to obtain and sustain our fresh anointing.

[5] And when the ark of the covenant of the LORD came into the camp, all Israel shouted with a great shout, so that the Earth rang again. [6] And when the Philistines heard the noise of the shout, they said, What meaneth the noise of this great shout in the camp of the Hebrews? And they understood that the ark of the Lord was come unto the camp. [7] And the Philistines were afraid, for they said God is come into the camp. And they said Woe unto us! For there hath not been such a thing heretofore.

[8] Woe unto us! Who shall deliver us out of the hand of these mighty Gods that smote the Egyptians with all the plagues of the wilderness.

—1 Samuel 4:5-8 (KJV)

The Philistines were frightened by their recollection of stories about God's intervention for Israel when they left Egypt. But Israel had turned away from God and now clung to only a form of godliness, a symbol of former victories. The Philistines then pushed past their fear and mercilessly slaughtered over thirty thousand Israelites and captured the Ark.

People, churches, and organizations often try to live on the memories of God's blessings. The Israelites wrongly assumed that since God had given them victory in the past, He would do it again, even though, in their hearts, Israel knew it had strayed far from God.

Today, as in the Old Testament, spiritual victories come through a consistent and continually renewed relationship with God. We dare not live off the past. We must keep our relationship with God new and fresh and flourishing.

We need to develop more consistency in our prayer life, in expressing our love of and for Christ, and in our faith. In doing so, we will ultimately lean not on our own understanding, but in all our ways we will gratefully begin to acknowledge Him. Prov. 3:6

[11] Wherefore the Lord said unto Solomon, Foreasmuch as this is done of thee, and thou has not kept my covenant and my statutes, which I have commanded thee, I will surely rend the kingdom from thee, and will give it to thy servant. [12] Notwithstanding in thy days I will not do it for David thy father's sake: but I will rend it out of the hand of thy son. [13] Howbeit I will not rend away all the kingdom; but will give it to one; but will give one tribe to thy son for

David my servant's sake, and for Jerusalem's sake which
I have chosen.

—1 Kings 11:11-13 (KJV)

During this juncture of the Bible, we learn that Solomon's powerful and glorious kingdom could have been blessed for all time; instead, it was approaching its end. Solomon had God's promises, guidance, and answers to prayer, and yet he allowed sin to remain all around him. Eventually, it corrupted him so much that he was no longer interested in the God of his paternal father David, or Abraham, Isaac, and Jacob.

Although Solomon had built his kingdom foundation on God, he lacked consistency and did not follow through in his later years. He allowed his many wives to worship other gods, and, as a result, Solomon lost everything. Additionally, Solomon unwittingly set up his children for a hereditary curse.

It is not enough to get off to a right start in building our lives on God's principles; we must endure with God to the end. God must control our lives from start to finish. I am as guilty as anybody is in this regard. I can't count the times I got in God's way by attempting to assist Him. I had to learn that God does not need my help to fix my problems; however, I can't do anything without His help. The Church needs Spiritual CPR!

The counsel of the Lord standeth forever, the thoughts to
all generations.

—Psalm 33:11 (KJV)

God's plan stands forever! Have you, like me, ever been frustrated by inconsistencies we see in others and even in ourselves? God is completely trustworthy, and His intentions never change. There is a promise that all good and perfect gifts come to us from the Creator who never changes. In the midst of the storm, when you wonder if there is anyone in whom you can trust, remember that God is completely consistent. Let Him counsel you, for He is a wonderful counselor. Seek Him for refuge, for the name of the Lord is a Strong Tower. Seek Him for comfort, for He is the Prince of Peace.

In his letter to the Philippians, Paul urges us to press toward the mark for the prize of the high calling of God in Christ Jesus. ^{Php. 3:14} So, not only must we be *consistent*, but we also must be *persistent*. Our best examples of persistence come from God's own example toward us.

PERSISTANCE

Wherefore I will yet plead with you, saith the Lord, and with your children's children will I plead.

—Jeremiah 2:9 (KJV)

God will never cease to plead with us because His love persists, even when we don't deserve it. I believe that God does this because He knows just how much we will lose if we fail to respond to His love. Eternity is a long, long time without Him. We must persistently press to respond to His pleas, to give ourselves wholeheartedly to God.

The word *plead* is often used in legal contexts. Like a plaintiff in a court case, I believe that God will bring charges against His wayward people. God is both the offended plaintiff and the divine judge before whom Israel (His chosen people) has no defense. Let us not be caught defenseless before God on Judgment Day.

And he said let me go for the day breaketh. And he said, I will not let thee go, except thou bless me.

—**Genesis 32:26 (KJV)**

The story of Jacob wrestling with the angel, whom I believe was the pre-incarnate Christ, is one of my favorites in the Bible. Even though he was enduring the affliction of a dislocated hip, Jacob continued his wrestling match all night, determined to be blessed. He was persistent. God encourages persistence in ALL areas of our lives, including the spiritual.

Strong character results from struggling under tough conditions. God wants you to have the blessing that you're pursuing, but you've got to go through some things for Him to know that you will worship the gift Giver and not worship the gift!

> Then the Lord said unto Moses, Go in unto Pharaoh, and tell him, Thus saith the Lord God of the Hebrews, Let my people go, that they may serve me.
>
> —Exodus 9:1 (KJV)

At this passage in the Bible, it was the fifth time that God had sent Moses back to Pharaoh with the demand "Let my people go!" Moses may have been tired and discouraged by this time, but he continued to be obedient.

Can you imagine that? The fifth time that Moses had to go before Pharaoh! This was the same Pharaoh that let jealousy fuel hatred towards Moses. This was the same Pharaoh that had Moses banished from Egypt. This was the same Pharaoh that could've had Moses beheaded the first time he came before him. And now, here it was the fifth time that God had instructed Moses to go before Pharaoh with the same demand.

How many times have we come to the crossroads of a personal conflict or test in our lives that we can't seem to pass? No matter how uncomfortable or difficult it may actually be, when we know what is right to do, we must be persistent, and we mustn't give up. As Moses discovered, *delayed* does not necessarily mean *denied*, and persistence is eventually rewarded.

> Ask and it shall be given you; seek and ye shall find; knock,
> and it shall be opened unto you: For everyone that asketh
> receiveth; and he that seeketh findeth; and to him that
> knocketh it shall be opened.
>
> —Matthew 7:7-8 (KJV)

Jesus tells us to persist in pursuing God. People often give up after a few half-hearted efforts to seek the Lord and conclude that God cannot be found. But knowing God takes faith, focus, and follow-through, and Jesus gives us a blessed assurance that our efforts will be rewarded.

We can't give up in our efforts to seek God. We must continue to persistently ask Him for more knowledge, more patience, more wisdom, more love, and more understanding. The Bible says that you have not because you ask not. [Jas. 4:2] We must know beyond a shadow of a doubt that He will reward them that diligently seek Him. [Heb. 11:6]

RESISTANCE

> For it came to pass, when Solomon was old, that his wives
> turned away his heart after other gods: and his heart was
> not perfect with the LORD his God, as was the heart of
> David his father.
>
> —1 Kings 11:4 (KJV)

King Solomon handled great pressures in running his government, but he could not handle the pressure from his wives, who wanted him to worship their gods. In marriage and other close relationships, it is often difficult to resist the pressure to compromise. Our feelings of love lead us to identify with the desires of those we care about most. Faced with such pressure, Solomon first resisted it, maintaining pure faith. Then he tolerated a more widespread practice of idolatry. Finally, he himself became involved in idolatrous worship. He rationalized away the potential danger to himself and his kingdom. Quite simply, when he failed to resist, he and his kingdom eventually failed to exist.

The Word teaches us how to make resisting temptation easier because you learn that once temptation strikes, it is already too late for us to ask for advice. When the sensation of desire is fully activated, your flesh doesn't want advice—your flesh wants satisfaction. Hello, somebody.

The best time to learn the dangers and potential destruction of going after forbidden sex, secret love, or carnal cravings (or anything else that is harmful to God's temple, our bodies) is long before the temptation comes.

> [11] And thou mourn at the last, when thy flesh and thy body are consumed, [12] And say, How have I hated instruction, and my heart despised reproof; [13] And have not obeyed the voice of my teachers, nor inclined mine ear to them that instructed me!
>
> **—Proverbs 5:11-13 (KJV)**

We can make the correct decision if we do what we've been taught. There is a saying that notes, "Once you know better, you ought to do better." I once heard the powerful Evangelist Shepherd Mother Cordelia Wallace, of the Agape Christian Fellowship of Brooklyn, New York, say, "Just do what the Bible told you."

No matter how you best receive it, know that resistance is easier if the decision has already been made. Don't wait to see what happens. Prepare for temptation by deciding, in advance, to follow Jesus' example of when Satan himself confronted him. Know how you will react when temptation confronts you.

As a basketball official, one of the best pieces of advice I ever received was from veteran NBA official Tom Washington. Tom wrote an article that was dealing with mental pre-game preparation. On the subject of coaches, Tom said know, going into the game, that most coaches are going to question your calls. His advice was to know how you would react to them once they did.

As simple as this sounds, I was a 12-year veteran at the time I read that, and I had never prepared myself mentally for that inevitable occurrence. I'm not talking about having a pocket full of brilliant one-liners *à la* Rodney Dangerfield, but being mentally prepared in advance for something that you know will happen.

As Christians carrying the blood-stained banner, we know that we are going to be tempted by the devil. I have failed countless tests in my flesh because I attempted to fight back after I was attacked. There is no way to prepare for war once the war has begun. You must prepare for warfare during times of peace. How are you preparing your resistance?

I believe that the strength of the church is determined by each individual member's relationship with God. I believe that we all must remain prepared, by a consistent attitude of prayer and worship, to be used by God. We'll never know when God may call us to perform a miracle in His name.

We can't afford to tell a drug addict to "hold on, let me go into prayer, and I'll get back to you in a few days." We can't afford to tell someone on their sick bed to "hold on while I call my Bishop and they'll schedule an appointment to come and lay hands on you so you can be healed." God is looking for someone who is willing to avail themselves to be used.

Remember that if you're in Christ, it's never too late for spiritual CPR. It's never too late to continue what the Lord has begun in you. If God thought enough of you to allow you to receive this awesome revelation, then you should have enough confidence in Him to know that He doesn't make mistakes. Just be consistent, persistent, and resistant, and I'm convinced that the Lord will use you mightily.

CHAPTER 13:

THE TIME IS NOW

Several Gospel songwriters have scribed the phrases, "Send me, I'll go," and "Where you lead me, I will follow," and "I will go in Jesus' name." These phrases all refer to one's willingness to be a disciple for Christ. Webster's dictionary defines a disciple as one who accepts and assists in spreading the Gospel of another.

However, the root word for *disciple* actually means 'to learn'. Let's focus on the root, meaning that if a disciple is a learner, then he must be willing to follow both the teachings and the teacher. Hello, somebody!

Let's explore the Word of God found in the Gospel of Matthew:

> [18] Now when Jesus saw great multitudes about him, he gave commandment to depart unto the other side. [19] And a certain scribe came, and said unto him, Master, I will follow thee whithersoever thou goest. [20] And Jesus saith unto him, The foxes have holes, and the birds of the air have nests; but the Son of man hath not where to lay his head. [21] And another of his disciples said unto

him, Lord, suffer me first to go and bury my father. [22] But Jesus said unto him, Follow me; and let the dead bury their dead.

—Matthew 8:18-22 (KJV)

Here Jesus gives us two examples of true tests of discipleship. In the first example Jesus lets a scribe know that the 'Son of man' has nowhere to lay His head. Jesus is telling this young man, "You are welcome to come and follow Me, but know what you are getting into. For I, the Son of man, have nowhere to lay My head."

In essence, what Jesus is saying is: "Count the cost, young man. Examine yourself before I grant you what you think you desire. Know that in order to be a true disciple, you have to give up this present life as you now know it, to receive the reward of life everlasting. Know that if you are compelled to carry My cross, you will be ridiculed, falsely accused, and forsaken by those who once claimed they loved you.

"Know that this road won't be easy and that you will face trials and tribulations for My name's sake. You must be willing to abandon the familiar comfort zone that you now embrace as well as all your earthly possessions. Yes, the cost is great, but the reward is a high throne in glory."

Jesus wants to know, are you willing to pay the price? We know that we can count on Jesus, but the question is, does Jesus know that He can count on you? For a moment, place yourself in the shoes of the scribe. Are we willing to give up all our earthly possessions? *This man is telling me that if I follow Him, I don't know where I will sleep.* My bedroom set may not be new, and I don't know about you, but I still enjoy sleeping in it! Hello, somebody!

In the second example, another of Jesus' would-be disciples asks if he could first go and bury his father, who more than likely was ailing. I believe that the man's request was a simple plea to share in his natural father's last moments on Earth and receive his due inheritance. However, to Jesus, his request was conditional. The man was willing to serve Jesus, but on his own terms or conditions. He had a "Yes, Lord!" spirit but was willing to serve Jesus only if he could first go and get his business straight.

How many of us are unaware that we are serving God conditionally or that we are willing to serve but only *after* we can get our business straight? Or *after* we stop using drugs, *after* we stop our lustful affair, *after* we pay off our new home or car and give up our second and third jobs so that we'll have time to become a real church member instead of just a churchgoer? Or how about *after* we make sure that our entire family is saved. Oh, yeah, and *after* I find my soul mate, then we'll be ready to serve Christ together, praise God!

But Jesus' response was simple and to the point. He said, "Follow me, and let the dead bury the dead." As harsh as this sounds, I don't believe that Jesus was trying to be harsh or inconsiderate. I believe that Jesus was just trying to emphasize that the time to be about My Heavenly Father's business was now! Now more than ever is the time that we so-called disciples of Christ must be about our Heavenly Father's business. Now is the time that we need to make God's business the number one priority in our lives.

Now is the time that we need to get in a hurry to do that which God has not just called us but ordained us to do. Now is the time that we need to get past the inconvenience of serving God by properly prioritizing ministry as the single most important thing in our lives. Now is the time for us to die daily to the flesh, [1 Cor. 15:31] so that God, the author and finisher of our faith, [Heb. 12:2] can be glorified!

In fact, most of us should have been doing this from day one of our salvation, but since we can't change our past, we must know that God allows U-Turns. So, now is the acceptable time to turn around and begin doing just that. In actuality, though, this is no more than our reasonable service. [Rom. 12:1]

When we crucify our flesh, ^{Gal. 5:24} surrender our will, and submit to God's will, then we will activate the power of Jesus' prayer to God, in which He said, "Give us this day our daily bread...." ^{Mat. 6:11}

Part of our "daily bread" entails us getting the benefit of God loading us up daily with, first and foremost, new mercies!!!! ^{Ps. 68:19} Oooooohhh!!! Let me stop here for a moment! I'm feeling this seed blooming in my spirit! In fact, I'm preaching myself happy!

David, in the book of Psalms, tells us of God's mercy when he says that "Great is thy mercy toward me" (Psalm 86:13, KJV), "God is plenteous in mercy" [Psalm 86:5,15; 103:8 (KJV)], and "His mercy endureth forever!" (over 30 times).

You see, we who have been born again need to know beyond a shadow of a doubt that if it had not been for God's mercy, then surely God could've allowed us to be destroyed in our mess. But because of His grace and mercy, we are given yet another opportunity to get our acts together. In my spirit, I can feel First Lady Miles proclaiming, "Get ready for double for your trouble!"

Also, because God is an omniscient God—meaning that He knows all even before it happens—He knows that we are going to be spiritually attacked when we follow Him and that sometimes we are going to stumble, so He loads us up daily with new mercies! New mercies for the little things; like when I was headed to a new job in Washington D.C. and my car began to malfunction on the highway. I just happened to be near an exit that happened to be next to a shop where I could get it fixed, and I coasted right there, got my car repaired just as they opened, and I still made it to the job location on time.

Or the bigger things, like when you didn't have any money and your rent was due and you received that '5 Days Pay Or Quit' notice. Then miraculously, in the 24th hour before the notice went into effect, God made a way for you to get it paid. That was His new mercy! The mercy that He loads the faithful up with daily!

When we realize that the time is now to serve God with our whole hearts and then worship Him in spirit and in truth, ^{Jn. 4:23-24}

then God becomes our 'Right Now God'! We get the benefits because He loads us up daily! God gets the glory when His will is fulfilled through our lives! And, best of all, when we get to heaven, we get our true reward!

However, we must serve Him unconditionally. We cannot afford to let anything come between our Savior and us. We've got to get in a hurry, people. Souls are being lost daily because we so-called disciples are not prepared to lead them to Christ. If we haven't done it already, let's start today. The time is now.

The time is now for us to prioritize God as the single most important thing in our lives. The time is now for us to speak to the mountain in our lives and believe that by faith that mountain will be moved! Mat. 17:20, 21:21; Mk. 11:23 The time is now for us to go into hospitals and not pray so loud that we get thrown out, but to lay hands on the sick and believe that God will heal them. The time is now for us to call out to the dead and command Lazarus to get up! Jn. 11:43 The time is now to know that we can trust in the Lord, but the question remains, can our Lord trust in us?

CHAPTER 14:
IN GOD'S WAITING ROOM

The motivation for this chapter came during a period in my life when it seemed that I was definitely still in-between the blessings of God. I found myself laid off from the job which God had blessed me with, and I began to examine everything around me to ensure that I wasn't unwittingly doing something to offend God and hinder my blessings.

As I submersed myself in God's Word, I was Spirit-led to the 27th Psalm. I began reading this Psalm aloud several times a day. Then the Lord led me to the anointed teachings of the great Evangelist Joyce Myers. At the time that Joyce's message was sown into my spirit, I received the revelation that I was definitely in God's Waiting Room.

PSALM 27 (KVJ)

[1] The LORD is my light and my salvation; whom shall I fear? the LORD is the strength of my life; of whom shall I be afraid?

[2] When the wicked, even mine enemies and my foes, came upon me to eat up my flesh, they stumbled and fell.

[3] Though an host should encamp against me, my heart shall not fear: though war should rise against me, in this will I be confident.

[4] One thing have I desired of the LORD, that will I seek after; that I may dwell in the house of the LORD all the days of my life, to behold the beauty of the LORD, and to inquire in his temple.

[5] For in the time of trouble he shall hide me in his pavilion: in the secret of his tabernacle shall he hide me; he shall set me up upon a rock.

[6] And now shall mine head be lifted up above mine enemies round about me: therefore will I offer in his tabernacle sacrifices of joy; I will sing, yea, I will sing praises unto the LORD.

[7] Hear, O LORD, when I cry with my voice: have mercy also upon me, and answer me.

[8] When thou saidst, Seek ye my face; my heart said unto thee, Thy face, LORD, will I seek.

[9] Hide not thy face far from me; put not thy servant away in anger: thou hast been my help; leave me not, neither forsake me, O God of my salvation.

[10] When my father and my mother forsake me, then the LORD will take me up.

[11] Teach me thy way, O LORD, and lead me in a plain path, because of mine enemies.

[12] Deliver me not over unto the will of mine enemies: for false witnesses are risen up against me, and such as breathe out cruelty.

[13] I had fainted, unless I had believed to see the goodness of the LORD in the land of the living.

[14] Wait on the LORD: be of good courage, and he shall strengthen thine heart: wait, I say, on the LORD.

David knew from experience what it meant to wait on the Lord. He had been anointed king at the age of 16 but didn't become king until he was 30. Can you imagine that? How many of us can be granted any position of authority, let alone a kingship, and then serve patiently until we receive it? I can't begin to understand that level of humility!

Yet, while David was in God's waiting room, an initially kind King Saul invited David into the palace. Then, it was a jealous King Saul who chased him through the wilderness, trying to kill him. Nonetheless, David had to wait on God for the fulfillment of his promise to reign. David didn't attempt to fix his situation himself. He never plotted to kill Saul. In fact, he served Saul with his whole heart. And even later, after becoming king, David was again chased by his rebellious son, Absalom.

David knew that sometimes we have to retreat from our everyday situations until God instructs us and directs our path. Hello, somebody. It doesn't mean that we're running because we'd lose the battle, only that we're retreating in obedience and submission to the will of God. Sometimes, if we fight right then, innocent bystanders will become casualties of our war.

In today's microwave society, waiting on God is never easy. There are times when it seems that He isn't answering our prayers or doesn't understand the urgency of our situation. That kind of carnal thinking implies that God is not in control or is not a fair God. But I'm here to tell you that we serve a fair and just God. God's word says that His time is not our time. God has repeatedly proven that He is always worth waiting for. The 27th through the 31st chapters of Isaiah call for us to wait because often God uses waiting to refresh, renew, realign, and reassign us.

Again, I don't know about you, but I need to be refilled with another dose of the Holy Ghost. I need to be fire-baptized and filled again, and again, and again. So, I will rejoice while I'm in God's waiting room. I will delight in Him while I'm dwelling in His presence. I'm excited knowing that He's equipping me for my next assignment.

And while I'm waiting, I will bless the Lord at all times, and His praises shall continually be in my mouth. ^{Ps. 34:1} I know that what God has for me is for me, and if I continue to diligently seek Him, He will reward me in my due season!

In times of stress, in times of trials, and in times of tribulations, total dependence on God requires our complete, first fruit, commitment.

Some people believe that if we could understand God's timing, then we could better cooperate with His plan for our lives. As I mentioned earlier, I've already tried that, and it didn't work for me! My Biblical justification for staying out of God's business is found in Isaiah 55:8 (KJV), where it says "my thoughts are not your thoughts, neither are your ways my ways." We must realize that we don't know God's timing for us, so we must be content to just know the One who does know.

If we're going to walk right with Him and enjoy His blessings, then we must learn to let God be God. Therefore, how can we better cooperate with the Master than by getting out of His way and taking a seat in God's waiting room?

In today's age of rapid technology, we Christians can find it so difficult to wait patiently for God to act when we want our change right away. But God promises that if we submit to His timing, then He will honor us. Peter said to "Humble yourselves therefore under the mighty hand of God, that He may exalt you in due time." [1 Pet. 5:9] This passage continues to convict me.

Now pastoring a growing ministry, I've found it sometimes difficult to wait as the Lord of the Harvest sends new workers into our church. I've found it challenging to watch some members repeatedly struggle with the same issues, challenges, and setbacks. I had to learn to treasure patience while in the waiting room of the Lord!

Before I began pastoring, and before I served as State President of Evangelism, a prophet of God sensed my impatience with not being recognized. So, he pulled me to the side and told me, "You have been blessed by God, and you don't need a title to be used by God. Remember that Isaiah was never called but simply made himself available to God to be used."

I understood that this prophet was not telling me to ignore God's protocol and start operating as I saw fit when I saw fit. No, what he was telling me was, *don't let a title stop you from fulfilling your Godly assignment.*

Philippians 4:6 instructs us to be anxious for nothing. That nothing means your new car, your new home, your Elder's license, your new job, as well as your soul mate and spouse. That nothing even means that book you know God told you to write. Hello, somebody!

Therefore, we must be patient, steadfast, immovable, always abiding in Him. We must be continually doing the work God has given us to do and allow God to choose the best time to manifest the change of our circumstances. We must allow God to be the gentleman that He is and open the door that He desires us to enter. Don't be like Mustang Sally and sling the door open for yourself. Let God get the door in *His* time when *He* sees fit.

Why is that so hard for us to do in the Spirit realm when we do it in the natural every day? When you're sick, you go to the doctor. You sign in with the receptionist, and then you have a seat in the doctor's waiting room. You don't know how long it's going to take to see the doctor, but you wait patiently, because you believe that when the doctor finally sees you, he's going to fix whatever is ailing you. And we do it! We do it, and most often we don't complain. And, in addition to that, we pay the doctor ridiculous amounts of money for their services.

And all the doctors can do is diagnose and operate, when it is only God that can heal us! Only God can reverse inoperable conditions! Only God can say when our life is over! But we don't want to tarry in God's waiting room. God has never sent us a bill for His services, yet we often grumble and complain while He's fixing us.

All He wants us to do is stand still and know that He is God! Ps. 46:9 Simply know that He loves us and broods over us like a hen over her chicks. Mat. 23:37; Lk. 13:34 That He upholds us, and even though we may slip, He won't let us lay disabled in our mess.

It's not like that commercial when the elderly person falls and then calls for help, saying that I've fallen and I can't get up! God always gives us the opportunity to take up our bed of affliction and walk. He gives us another opportunity to repent, another opportunity to be restored, and another opportunity to be made whole.

But it is in His waiting room where He commands our full attention. It's in His waiting room where all things work together for the good of those that love the Lord and to those who are called according to His purpose. Rom. 8:28 *His* purpose, not our purpose! How can we inherit the promise if we're not willing to fulfill His purpose?

When Jesus was instructing the disciples how to pray and He said, "Thy will be done," Mat. 66:10; Lk. 11:2 He wasn't talking about *our* will. He was talking about *God's* will! The Bible says that the steps of a righteous man are ordered by God. Ps. 37:23 It doesn't say, "go and do whatever you want to do, and then God will bless you." No! We have got to learn how to do what God is *blessing!* The only way we can do that is to be still and hear from God.

When we prove that we love Him as Job did, while our entire world is being shattered around us, that's when He'll bless us with the double for our trouble. That's when He'll anoint us with the fruits of His Spirit. That's when our ministries will be revealed. That's when His awesome power and miracles will manifest all around us for everyone to see without us uttering a single word! That's when His abundant windows of blessings will begin flowing and overtake us. That's when our children's children will be left a prince's and a princess' inheritance!

When we dwell in God's waiting room and praise Him for who He is, not what He's done, and unconditionally learn to trust Him, then will joy come in the morning. [Ps. 30:5] And morning is not necessarily in the 'a.m.'. Morning is when we wake up!

These are a few Scriptures that encouraged me while I was waiting:

> **Psalm 37:7,9 (KJV)** Rest in the LORD, and wait patiently for Him... [9] those that wait upon the LORD, they shall inherit the Earth

> **Psalm 37:34 (KJV)** Wait on the LORD, and keep His way, and He shall exalt thee

> **Job 14:14 (KJV)** All of my appointed life will I wait, till my change come

> **Psalm 62:1 (KJV)** Truly my soul waiteth upon God: from Him cometh my salvation

> **Psalm 130:5 (KJV)** I wait for the LORD, my soul doth wait, and in His word do I hope

> **Proverbs 27:18 (KJV)** He that waiteth on his master shall be honoured

> **Acts 1:4 (KJV)** wait for the promise of the Father

> **Isaiah 40:31 (KJV)** But they that wait upon the LORD shall renew their strength; they shall mount up with wings as eagles; they shall run, and not be weary; and they shall walk and not faint.

I had to learn that once I progressed from being an infant in the Lord, He wasn't going to tend to me every time I started crying. God is the one who instilled paternal instincts in us. He knows that there are times when we are growing in Him, when we have to learn patience, perseverance, and longsuffering! He knows that it may be uncomfortable and downright painful, but it's for our own good.

God has not forsaken us; He is merely equipping us before anointing us for our next assignment. So, take a seat, be patient, and hold on to your faith. You're in God's waiting room, and there is no more exciting place to be!

PART 4:

PROSPERED

CHAPTER 15:

SELF, GET OUT OF MY WAY AND STOP HOLDING ME BACK

If we ever were to come to grips with the person in the mirror, the reality is that the reason that most of us are living beneath our God-intended privilege is because we are holding ourselves back. When you are living in God's will, there is no one powerful enough to keep you from fulfilling your potential and walking in your divine destiny. So, what is it then that is holding up our blessings? The major prophet Jeremiah gave the following revelation:

> Your iniquities have turned away these things, and your sins have withholden good things from you.
>
> —Jeremiah 5:25 (KJV)

In order to better understand and heed the prophet's words, we need to grasp the background of what was transpiring when Jeremiah made this statement.

In the 5th chapter of Jeremiah, the Lord instructs Jeremiah to go unto the streets of Jerusalem and find just one righteous man beside himself. Much like the Lord agreed to spare Sodom and Gomorrah for ten righteous people, [Gen. 18:32] here He asks Jeremiah to find just one righteous man besides himself. God tells Jeremiah that "if there be any man that executeth judgment and seeketh the truth, then He will pardon it [Jerusalem]." (Jeremiah 5:1, KJV)

You see, judgment and truth were often used in the Old Testament as a standard of righteousness. They were found not only in the perfection of God but also were supposed to characterize the believer's life. This is so because you cannot call yourselves true believers if you are not executing Biblical judgment and seeking the Word of truth.

You may ask, "What do you mean, Mr. Preacher, by executing Biblical judgment?" My response would be to go to James 1:22 (KJV), where it says, "be ye doers of the word and not hearers only, deceiving your own selves."

That means, my good friend, don't sit up in church, hear the preached word, and still go to hell! All men certainly should avoid hell, but how can you justify sitting up in church and still going? You've got to take the Word of God literally and apply it to your lives. You can't let it come into one ear and go out the other. That's why David said in the book of Psalms, "Thy word have I hid in mine heart, that I might not sin against thee." (Psalm 119:11, KJV)

God hates sin and will not bless us in our sin. So, the Word comes not to condemn us, but to correct us. The Word comes to identify our sins, then to correct us, and then to guide us into the path of righteousness.

Know that you cannot microwave righteousness. Righteousness has got to slow-cook within so that it simmers in your spirit. But it's not the nature of man that he is made to wait. That's why the Bible extols the virtues of patience. That's why we've got to train our flesh because our flesh forever rages against our spirit. We've got to actually beat our flesh into submission. I don't know about you, but I'm sick and tired of being my own biggest nemesis. Somebody who agrees with me ought to stand up and holler, "Self, get out of my way and stop holding me back!"

The only way that we can beat our flesh into submission is by strengthening our Spirit Man. Right now, most of our flesh is like the cartoon character Bluto. It's overweight because it's overfed. It's volatile and ready to pounce on whatever it thinks it wants.

And our poor little Spirit Man is like Popeye. Arms like spaghetti, small and under-developed. The big bully Bluto just dominates us whenever he gets ready. But the Word of God is spinach to our spirit. Hello, somebody. And when we feast off the Word, then we become like Popeye after eating his spinach, and we're then able to beat our big, bad flesh into submission! If you want to take it one step further, you can say that ol' Olive Oil is our blessing that God has given us. Your flesh has just dominated your spirit and caused you to lose your blessing.

But when you have a daily diet of God's Word, you can pump up your Spirit Man and reclaim everything that your own silly self has caused you to lose. What was it that Popeye used to say? "That's all I can stands; I can't stands no more!"

When you begin to execute Biblical judgment, you can coast through trials and tribulations because your course is already charted. You know that when the storm winds are raging, you don't try to bring yourself out, but you *let go and let God*. You take your hands off your life's steering wheel and you switch on the autopilot. Then lights come on that all can see that say, "In God I Trust and All My Help Comes from the Lord."

When everything around you is crumbling and it seems that your world is in turmoil and you find yourself in what seems like a permanent state of being in-between blessings, you can still walk around with your head held high and a smile on your face, singing, *"I'm trusting in You, Lord; I'm trusting in You. You've been so faithful. You've been so true. You never fail me, but I've failed you. Please forgive me. I'm trusting in You."*

In doing this, you begin to elevate your faith to a higher level. Now you're ready to seek after the way of truth.

Deuteronomy 32:4 (KJV) says: *He is the rock, His work is perfect, for all His ways are judgement: a God of truth and without iniquity, just and right is He.*

Psalm 119:30 (KJV) says: *I have chosen the way of truth, thy judgements have I laid before me.*

Notice that it says "the *way* of truth" and not the *ways* of truth. It's not plural! That's because there's only one truth, and that one truth is the Word of God.

So, it's simple and clear: If you're seeking the truth, you've got to first seek God! You may say, "How can I seek God when He cannot be seen?" My answer will be to go to "the beginning" as described by the Apostle John, who says: *In the beginning was the Word, and the Word was with God and the Word was God.* (John 1:1, KJV)

So, to find the truth, you need to find God; and to find God, just look in the Word! To some of us, this might mean taking God from the shelf and dusting Him off. You may be surprised to know that He's been there all the time. We need to eat the Word and eat the Word and then eat it some more!

We need to take God's Word and hide it deep in our hearts until we become a Word sponge. When you're a Word sponge, whenever you're pressed, then out comes the Word. When the devil afflicts you with temptations of the flesh... out comes the Word. When your children are acting like they've lost their minds... out comes the Word. When your spouse is acting more like your adversary than the loving person you married... out comes the Word. When the enemy comes in like a flood... out comes the Word, and the Lord will raise up a standard against your adversaries, and no weapon formed against you shall prosper. (Isaiah 54:17, KJV)

The only way that we can be defeated is if we choose to defeat ourselves. So, self, get outta' my way and stop holding me back!

I am determined not to miss any more of God's blessings. I am committed to make my last bad decision, my LAST bad decision! I am convinced that I will no longer set my children and future grandchildren up for hereditary curses caused by my disobedience to God.

If we allow ourselves to continue to feed our flesh, then in our flesh we must die daily. We must continually lay aside the weight of our affliction. We must come to the realization that our flesh is insatiable! It will never be satisfied. When we give in to our flesh, it's like taking a hit of a crack pipe; one is too many and a thousand is not enough! Maybe your weakness is not in your flesh. Maybe you have a lying spirit. Maybe you have a rebellious spirit. Whatever your infirmity may be, don't continue to let it hinder you.

We need to speak to our secret sin and call it what it is: SIN! All of us have sinned and come short of the Glory of God! [Rom. 3:23] So let the Lord strengthen us where we are weak! Let the Lord build us up and make us strong! Let the Lord purge us from all unrighteousness! Then we can speak to the mountains in our lives, even those that were self-constructed. Then we can expose the enemy for the deceiver that he is.

In this the season of last and evil days, it is God's desire that we prosper. However, God is not a man that He would lie, [Num. 23:19] and He will not go against His own Biblical principles. Therefore, in order for us to prosper, we need to ensure that we are not the cause for us to be lacking. God says that "the wealth of the sinner is laid up for the just", [Prov. 13:22] but are we living a just and righteous life? Let's check ourselves so that we can correct ourselves. Then, and only then, we can keep ourselves from holding ourselves back.

CHAPTER 16:
DON'T GET STUCK IN YOUR STORM

At some time in our lives, we have all had to survive a stormy situation. I have found that the greater your storm, the greater your anointing. Hello, somebody! Often the enemy can recognize our divine destiny before we can. When this happens, Satan will not hesitate to try and derail you before you can reach your full potential.

There are other times that God will allow certain situations to engulf your life in order to perfect you for your ministerial assignment. There is no shortcut to greatness in God. Be not deceived: anointing is costly!

There are often painful lessons that we must learn. Like a mother eagle, God would not push us off a cliff without knowing that we could fly. Like a lioness, God would not leave us in the wild without knowing that we could hunt. God is omnipotent, so

He doesn't have to convince Himself of our outcome. God often allows us to be overcomers of our storms, so that we know that we can overcome!

If we were never sick, how would we know that God is a healer? The key is not to give up in the midst of our trials and tribulations. Know that they come to make us strong, to build our faith, and to convince us that "in all these things we are more that conquerors." (Romans 8:37, KJV) But we've got to be careful not to get caught in our storm.

This chapter revolves around the book of Job and how it was powerfully expounded upon by Bishop T.D. Jakes and sown into my spirit during a period when I desperately needed to be reminded and encouraged. I thank God for this revelation.

The story of Job is one of the most well-known throughout the Bible. It is also one of the most heavily debated and refuted by those who stoop to such. This is not surprising to me because there were so many spiritually significant things that happened in the life of Job that if believers would, by faith, embrace them, ALL our trials and tribulations would diminish in comparison. The book of James says that Job is an encouragement to believers who also suffer despite living righteous lives. [Jas. 5:11] Therefore, those who oppose the Kingdom of God would benefit greatly if the people of God would embrace doubt, which is the very opposite of faith, pertaining to brother Job.

There are some key points to remember about Job. Although Job was blessed before his affliction, he became twice as blessed when he overcame his storm. The Lord Himself described Job to Satan as being perfect (blameless) and upright and one that feared Him. Yet, when we examine Job, we see that he dealt with many tormented thoughts throughout his ordeal. The key is that although he wrestled internally, Job never sinned against God with his lips.

Job's friends questioned his walk with God. Not only did they accuse Job of secretly sinning against God, but they did so at a time when Job was at his lowest point. Has anyone ever been there? Job's understanding of God reflected the viewpoints of that time, which was that God was a moral judge who expected His people to live up to commonly accepted moral standards.

The consensus of the time was that God rewarded those who did so and punished those who did not. Job was deeply troubled because he could not explain his suffering. All Job knew and held on to was the fact that God was not punishing him for sin. Job endured many afflictions that lasted a very long time; however, the Lord didn't bring Job out of his storm until Job prayed for the very ones that falsely accused him. This, in itself, is an awesome lesson to the Church today!

So, what I ascertain from the life of Job is that we should never make a permanent decision over a temporary situation. In the midst of our mess, we need to stand still and see the salvation of God. You see, we must know and understand that it is not only Satan's desire to harm God's people, but it is his job. However, we must take comfort in knowing that God has placed a fence around us that no demon from hell, including Satan himself, can penetrate without God's permission.

No matter what we endure, we must continue to hold on to our integrity. Know that as children of God we are raw jewels, but when we go through the fire, then we come out as pure gold. Job said God "knoweth the way that I take: when He hath tried me, I shall come forth as gold." (Job 23:10, KJV) People, there is absolutely no need to get stuck in your storm.

To ensure that we don't get stuck in our storm, the following formula will allow us not to get in God's way but for God to bring us out at His time. Know that it is dangerous for anyone to "put God in a box" and to assume from what we know of Him that God must act in this way or that.

While we are in our storm...

WE MUST NEVER FORGET OUR PAST BLESSINGS! Remember the last time we were going through a storm and believe that if God brought us through that, then He will certainly bring us through this! Know that last week's test is this week's testimony! The enemy wants to distract you to the point that you can't see your way out of your mess. The enemy stirs up a swirl of confusion so that your relationship with God is hindered. But, precious hearts, be not dismayed. Know that "weeping may endure for a night, but joy cometh in the morning"! (Psalm 30:5, KJV) The joy of the Lord is our strength, and we should embrace that old testimonial song that says, "I get joy when I think about what He's done for me!"

WE MUST ENCOURAGE OURSELVES! Have you ever noticed that when you're really going through a little something-something, it turns into what I call "the pit experience"? What I mean by that is that you find yourself like Joseph, thrown into a pit by those closest to you, or possibly your own mis-doings. You find yourself in a position where there is no one to hear you but God. Don't get angry that your friends and family can't help you, but rejoice in the fact that God, the source of everything you need, is there with you and for you. Once you realize that, like David ultimately did, the only thing that's left is for you to encourage yourself! Know that if God brought you to it, then He'll certainly bring you through it! Know that self-encouragement, through the knowledge of who you are in God, is the shovel to dig your way out of your pit of despair.

WE MUST REMEMBER TO PRAISE HIM! Never, never, never let anything hinder you from offering the Lord your praise. And not just lip service, but the sincere, whole-hearted sacrifice of praise. Have you ever seen children praising God? Jesus said that out of the mouths of babes comes perfected praise. ^{Mat. 21:16} He's not just talking about young children but also those who are young in Christ, for it is they that are uninhibited with their praise. We've got to go back to where we didn't care who was around us or what they thought. We need to get back to our childlike mindset, that regardless of our situation or surroundings, we were going to praise our God.

When I was laid off from my job as a computer consultant, I had not returned to work in that capacity. During that storm, I was very careful not to let anything hinder my praise. In October of 2001, our church embarked on a "First Fruit Fast." For this fast, the church consumed only water and juice for the first three days of the month. On the second day of November, in the midst of my fast, I was at the computer and I noticed a few flashes of light in my eyes. I got up from the computer, and my left eye was responding as if a bright light was shining in it. Immediately, the devil began telling me that I just needed to eat something and everything would be OK. I shouted at Satan and told him that I would not come off this fast, even if I went blind. My eye then became covered with a dark lens, although it couldn't be seen; it was almost as if a cataract had formed over my left eye. I was scared and in pain. I put hot compresses on my eye, but it didn't help. I cried unto the Lord and asked Him what was wrong with me!

Several hours later, I went to our Friday night church service, not telling anyone there what I was dealing with, and early in the service, the Spirit of the Lord saturated and consumed the house. I knew that the water was troubled. I immediately began to praise the Lord like I'd lost my mind. I started running up and down the center aisle and then broke out in a King David victory dance. My eyes were closed, and I just kept thanking the Lord as tears began to fall. When I opened my eyes, the cataract or affliction I had endured was, miraculously, completely gone! Don't tell me what praise won't do! I'm a living witness that praise can deliver you out of any situation.

WE MUST OPERATE IN FAITH! Faith demands a sacrifice. Just like the "First Fruit Fast" just mentioned, God is excited when we give Him our first and our best. If it's not something of value to us, then we must be careful not to offer it to God. That's why a sacrifice of praise can be a validation of our faith. We must know and believe that our pain may be real, our debt may be real, and that our adversary is busy, but we must have unwavering faith to know that this is only a test and God is more than able to deliver us out of our mess. We must be careful not to build a house on the foundation of our trouble. The Israelites never built houses in the desert because they had faith that God was bringing them out. It's all right to pitch a tent, but always operate in faith and know that you don't have to dwell there.

WE MUST NEVER FORGET OUR PRAYERS! When you pray, God can move on your behalf. Prayer is powerful! Bishop T.D. Jakes says that prayer is "the breakfast of champions"! The Bible says "the prayers of a righteous man availeth much"! (James 5:16, KJV) Prayer allows God to make a way out of no way! Prayer, therefore, is a waymaker! Prayer will give you favor, and favor is truly greater than life! Too many times when we are going through a trial, we are tricked into turning away from prayer instead of turning to counsel with God. Too many times we entertain the counsel of the ungodly [Ps. 1:1] (or the almost saved) and we deny the very source from which all blessings flow. We need to be reminded that all our help comes from the Lord. [Ps. 121:2] It is often said that prayer is the single most powerful yet most underused weapon of the believer. What greater peace can be found than in the prayer of having a little talk with Jesus? I can't wait to hear Jabez give his testimony on the power of prayer!

WE MUST CONTINUE TO ESTABLISH THOSE AROUND US! Regardless of what we are going through, we cannot afford to break relationships and abandon those around us. We may not literally abandon them, but we can't afford to abandon them spiritually, physically, or mentally. Even if they are falsely accusing us. Even if they are plotting our destruction and mean us nothing but harm. The Bible calls for us to continue to establish them and pray for them as well. Even if we are constantly seeking the face of God, we cannot become so spiritual and heaven-bound that we are no earthly good to those around us.

We can't mistreat others because they are mistreating us. In fact, while we are going through, we must place ourselves under a spiritual, Biblically correct microscope. We must ensure that there is no sin in our lives, either sins of commission (willful) or sins of omission (neglecting to do that which we know is right), which would hinder God's will and timing for bringing us out of our dilemma.

We must continue to stand firm and faithfully serve in the positions that God has confidently assigned us. We cannot let our ministries suffer because of what we're going through. We must continue to praise and worship God; serve; encourage; and establish those—both the leaders and lay members—who labor among us. We cannot afford to allow ourselves to get stuck in our storm!

WE MUST NEVER LOOSE OUR PURPOSE IN THE MIDDLE OF OUR STORM! Know that it has always been God's purpose to bless us. Our God is a God of destiny, and He has predestined us to be blessed! We must know with the very fabric of our being that God has a purpose for our lives, and that He has more than equipped us with everything we need to fulfill our task. No matter how unpleasant our circumstances may become, we must find solace in knowing that one of the reasons God allows us to go through trouble is so He can give us the victory over and beyond what we've ever seen or imagined!

We must embrace the verse in Ephesians: "Now unto him that is able to do exceeding abundantly above all that we ask or think, according to the power that worketh in us." (Ephesians: 3:20, KJV) Paul's letter to the church at Ephesus is telling us that beyond ALL that we can ASK OR THINK, God will do exceeding and abundantly more!!! If you've never rejoiced over the Word of God, you ought to rejoice over that! Because, people, we can ask for some stuff! But God is telling us that not only will He give us much more than we can ask for, but also above and beyond anything that we can imagine!!!

Somebody needs to know that I imagined writing a message, but because of God's power that works in me, I'm authoring this book! Somebody needs to know that I've been financially bound to debt demons for most of my life, but God has already ordained and released my season to walk in prosperity! I have no idea of how much God is about to bless me, but all I know is that I'm holding on to His promise to fulfill my purpose!

If you had not been afflicted, then you could never have been perfected! Brothers and sisters, don't get stuck in your storm! Just keep telling yourself: *I'm coming out! God is bringing me out! And I'm gonna get double for my trouble!*

CHAPTER 17:

THE SET TIME IS COME

When exploring the Biblical teachings of prosperity, I found that there is no more anointed a teacher than Dr. Creflo Dollar. While studying one of his messages, Pastor Dollar began to sow this seed into my spirit. This was such an awesome word that it immediately began germinating in my fertile soil! Unmistakably, this was my season for its planting, and my time of harvest is near. I share with you now the revelation that I received.

Let's begin by examining two text Scriptures for confirmation, Numbers 13:30 and Psalm 102:13.

> And Caleb stilled the people before Moses, and said, Let us go up at once, and possess it; for we are well able to overcome it.
>
> —Numbers 13:30 (KJV)

This story is also one of my favorites. It's one of courage and bravery. It gives justification to embracing the mentality of an eagle and soaring alone, above the crowd. I love it because it speaks of embracing one's destiny.

The Newbury House Online Dictionary states that being able is as being skilled and competent as in: my wife is a very *able* teacher. The dictionary also states that *able* is having the *power to do* as in: after Jesus healed him, he was able to walk again. The definition further elaborates that being able is being *free to do* as in: I am *able and willing* to praise my God.

So, if we are skilled and competent, having the power and free to do, then what is our excuse for not fulfilling God's purpose for our lives? We've already begun to check ourselves so that we can correct ourselves. We've also yelled aloud, "Self, get outta my way and stop holding me back!" We're careful to not get stuck in our storm, so what's up?

When we, the saints of God, think of the word *able*, we should think of God, because we know that we serve a God who is able to do anything but fail. Where we often fail and mess up and postpone and even miss our blessings is when we neglect to realize that our "able" God has given us the same ability to be able to overcome anything and everything that we are faced with.

In Genesis 1:26 (KJV), God our Creator says, "Let us make man in our image....". So, if God created man in His image, He also gave man the ability to be able. Everyone reading this book ought to stand up and proclaim: I am ABLE to succeed! I am ABLE to live holy! I am ABLE to pray and not faint! I am ABLE to achieve life everlasting! I am ABLE to receive the wealth of the wicked! I am ABLE to be more than a conqueror! I am ABLE to be the head and not the tail! I am ABLE to prosper!

Now you really ought to stop and give God some praise. By being obedient and repeating those words, I see and hear shackles falling in my spirit. I feel deliverance is finally coming to someone that's been pressing for a while, wondering if their breakthrough would ever come! Thank You, Lord.

Getting back to the story, in the 13th chapter of Numbers, around 1406 BC—after their long journey from Egypt—the Israelites were now poised to enter the Promised Land. They were camped at Kadesh, an oasis in the desert bordering southern Canaan. The town of Rehob was about 250 miles to the north. The Lord instructed Moses to send some men to explore the land of Canaan, which He had earlier promised to the Israelites. The Lord told Moses to send from each ancestral tribe one of its leaders.

When Moses sent the twelve men to explore Canaan, he instructed them to see what the land is like and whether the people that live there are strong or weak, few or many. He also told them to find out what kind of land they live in and to do their best to bring back some of the fruit of that land. In other words, Moses sent his best crew to go and scope it out. So, the chosen dozen left Kadesh and explored the land from the Desert of Zin as far as Rehob and eventually came to Hebron. Hebron was Palestine's highest town, lying 3,040 ft above sea level in the Judean hills. History tells us that Abraham, Isaac, and Jacob were all buried at Hebron.

At the time of the Patriarchs, Hebron was just a trading place for shepherds and herdsman. But now, 400 years later, the explorers saw a large, fortified town that was the royal city of the Anakites. The Anakites were a race of giants! It was widely believed that Goliath was an Anakite who had sought refuge with the Philistines.

When the explorers reached the valley of Eschol, which was a little more than a hundred miles from Kanesh, they cut off a branch bearing a single cluster of grapes. The grapes were so large that, including some pomegranates and figs, it took two men to carry the fruit on a pole between them.

At the end of the forty days, the men returned from exploring the land. Ten of the twelve explorers gave Moses this same account, "We went into the land of which you sent us, and it does flow with milk and honey! Here is the fruit. But the people who live there are big and powerful, and the cities are fortified and very large. We even saw the descendants of Anak there. We can't attack those people, for they are much stronger than we are."

Now, it wasn't good enough that they gave Moses this account, but just like some church folk—I ain't talkin' about y'all that's reading this, but you know, some of those *other* church folk—they spread a bad report throughout the "church" (Israelites). They stirred up so much dissension between themselves that they were ready to abandon Moses and Aaron, choose another leader, and go back to Egypt!

Can you imagine that? They were so distressed that they believed that they would be better off in captivity! They were willing to go back to sure slavery or death! They obviously still had a slave's mentality! In the midst of all this confusion, two men who were among the chosen dozen that explored the land— Joshua, from Ephraim's tribe and Caleb, from Judah's tribe—took a stand and said, "Just hold on! The land we passed through and explored is exceedingly good. If the Lord is pleased with us, He will lead us into that land...."

Then God saw this as a teaching moment. I believe that when a teaching moment presents itself, it becomes an opportunity to give God some glory!

So, the glory of the Lord appeared and said to Moses, "How long will these people treat Me with contempt? Not one of you will enter the land I swore with uplifted hand to make your home except Caleb and Joshua. As for your children... I will bring them in to enjoy the land that you have rejected. But you and your bodies will fall in this desert."

And God smote the ten doubters and proclaimed that their children would be shepherds there for forty years, suffering for their unfaithfulness! In essence, their fear, doubt, and ignorance translated into a hereditary curse.

The rest of the story is in God's Word. Moses told the people what God had said, and they had a brief pity party. Then they decided that early the next morning they would attempt to fix their own dilemma and go up to the city in the mountains to take Canaan. So, here those fools took off trying to fix something that they obviously couldn't, and the Canaanites whooped their tail good and forced them to wander in the wilderness.

Why did God let His people get beat down, you might ask. It's because they weren't in God's will. Why weren't they in God's will, you might ask. Because they didn't go when God told them to go! We've got to realize that delayed obedience is DISOBEDIENCE!

Well, Brother Steve, you might say, what's that got to do with us here today? And what in the world does this have to do with my prosperity? Well, let's look at the moral of the story! Stay with me now and savor this gravy that's about to flow! I promise, we're gonna sop it up before we're through, but just savor it right now!

The Israelites' sin was to doubt the Word of God. God's punishment was to deny the Israelites the land that He had promised to them. If you still don't know how that applies to you today, then somebody needs to give you a mirror, because the person you'll see is one of those who think that yo' stuff don't stink! So, for yo' sake, 'cause I still love you, let me break it down.

1. **Doubt the word of God:** How many times have we, in our spirits or in our minds, secretly in a closet or blatantly in the open, or simply by our actions, doubted the Word of God? How many times have we failed to realize that doubt is the exact opposite of faith! And without faith it is impossible to please God! Heb. 11:6

2. **God punishes by denying the promise:** How many times have your blessings been turned away because of the sin of disobedience? Remember what Jeremiah 5:25 (KJV) says, "Your iniquities have turned away these things, and your sins have withholden good things from you."

But the good part about all this is that God had not—not back then nor now—abandoned His chosen people. Hello, somebody!

He's talking about us! We are His chosen people! I don't care how bad you think you're doing or how bad your situation seems, God has not abandoned you!

In this story, God flips the script and He renews His covenant with the next generation. They will eventually inherit the land that their disobedient parents rejected!!! Somebody reading this ought to get really happy and stand up and shout, *"The Set Time Is Come! And it's time to flip the script!"*

If that example isn't enough, then let's explore our second text Scripture:

> Thou shalt arise and have mercy upon Zion: for the time
> to favor her, yea, the set time, is come.
>
> —Psalm102:13 (KJV)

God will rise up and have mercy upon us, the righteous house of Zion. For it is not only our time, but it is our turn! The set time is come! If you believe what you're reading, then say seven times aloud, *"My set time is come!"*

Spiritually, seven is a number of great significance. The world thinks that it's a lucky number when you're gambling shooting craps, but we, the saints of the Most High God, know that the number seven is a holy number! Seven is God's number for completion and perfection. God is completing His work in the perfecting of the Church! Colossians 4:12 (KJV) says "that ye may stand perfect and complete in all the will of God!" And it is the will of God in heaven that we PROSPER!

Check out Nehemiah 2:20 and examine what it says:

> Then answered I them and said unto them, The God of
> heaven, he will prosper us; therefore we his servants will
> arise and build...
>
> —Nehemiah 2:20 (KJV)

As my man Crefflo might say, "Aw, we're working this thing now." Let's jump back over to Psalm 102. The 16th verse says, "When the LORD shall build up Zion, He shall appear in His glory." Colossians 1:27 talks about God's riches of the glory. You see, the glory of God is God's manifested presence in blessings, in healing, in His anointing, in our prosperity!

So, in Psalm102:16 (KJV), it says, "When the LORD shall build up Zion, He shall appear in His glory." Then in the 18th verse (KJV) it says, "This shall be written for the generation to come: and the people which shall be created shall praise the Lord." Are we not the generation to come? If so, then shall we praise the Lord? Shall we praise Him in the firmament of His might?

We are that generation, and our set time is come! Like Moses and the Israelites, some of our parents, our grandparents, and our great-grandparents have been disobedient and have doubted the Word of God. Our ancestors have wandered in the wilderness of America, and other nations, long enough. God has delivered us out of the bondage of slavery and has made you and me able in every sense of the word. The set time is come for God to transfer the wealth of the wicked. The set time is come for us to shed the mentality of just enough and embrace our abundance of more than enough!

> Evil pursueth sinners: but to the righteous good shall be repayed. A good man leaveth an inheritance to his children's children: and the wealth of the sinner is laid up for the just.

> **—Proverbs 13:21-22 (KJV)**

Make no mistake about it, prosperity is a spirit that we must learn to embrace. We must speak to it daily! We must call it and command that spirit to embrace us! But before the spirit of prosperity can engulf us, we must first shed the spirit of poverty!

These two spirits cannot coexist within us! You must obey one or the other.

If you think that we don't house the spirit of poverty, I'll share a seven-step test. If any of the seven applies to you, then you need to shed the spirit of poverty before you can embrace the spirit of prosperity!

1. You make excuses for where you currently are financially.

2. You are critical of those who teach and preach about prosperity.

3. You don't think that a man or woman of God should be prosperous.

4. If you begin to question, "Does it take all that giving?"

5. If you are afraid to give under the direction of the Holy Spirit and give whatever It tells you to give.

6. If you govern your finances with a lack of God.

7. If you are suspicious of every man of God that comes around you, especially during offering time.

If you have failed any of these test steps, then you are operating under the spirit of poverty. Now, God is not revealing this fresh *rhema* Word to condemn us, but His Word has come to correct us and to get us on the right path to our newfound prosperity.

After the spirit of poverty has been shed and the spirit of prosperity has been embraced, God will bless us. But let me warn you, saints, for in the midst of your initial blessing, you may find a test attached to it. You see, I believe that the power to get and keep our wealth lies in the spirit of firstfruit offerings. Firstfruit offerings embrace the spirit of Abel. It's when you offer your first and your best!

And the first ripe fruit should go to your pastor. You may think that my pastor conspired to convince you of this, so don't take my word for it. Go to the book of Ezekiel:

And the first of all the firstfruits of all things, and every oblation of all, of every sort of your oblations, shall be the priest's: ye shall also give unto the priest the first of your dough, that he may cause the blessing to rest in thine house.

—Ezekiel 44:30 (KJV)

Now, I don't know about you, but I want my entire house to be blessed! I don't just want to get a blessing, but I want to keep my blessings flowing! Why? Because the set time is come! People, this is our due season! This is our time for our households to be blessed! Our children will be blessed! Our dog will be blessed! When you get a housekeeper, your housekeeper will be blessed! Why? Because the set time is come!

I believe that God is sick and tired of us holding up holy hands and having empty pockets. God is about to bless those who are in His will. God will bless us not only for ourselves but so that we may bring our blessings into the storehouse and then be a blessing to His people.

NOW THANK GOD FOR YOUR PROSPERITY!

CHAPTER 18:
PRAYER, PROPHECY AND PRAISE PRODUCE PROSPERITY

As we endeavor to not get stuck in our storms, we become very sensitive to our behavior while we're in the midst. The Bible says in Psalm23:5 that God will prepare a table for us in the presence of our enemies. What exactly does that mean? I believe that God is telling us that when you are in His divine will and you find trouble on every hand, don't despair, but resume your posture of prayer and praise, and He will bless you tremendously right where you are, in the presence of your enemies.

Where we as Christians struggle is by neglecting to stay spiritually focused on the Lord in the entanglement of our mess. We must know and acknowledge that what we are going through is very real, but we should not expect a natural cure for our spiritual dilemma. There is nothing that happens in the life of the believer that doesn't have spiritual significance. So, even though we're about to be consumed, we need to stop like David did and give God some praise!

We must become oblivious to the outwardly obvious and concentrate completely on the person who preordained the promise. We must draw from that which has been spiritually instilled in us. We must utilize our spiritual blinders and block out all distractions that would keep us out of God's presence.

When we embrace the spiritual 20/20 vision of God's true prophets, then we have no recourse but to overcome and prosper. What I call spiritual 20/20 vision is based in the Word of God found in Second Chronicles 20:20 (KJV), which proclaims: "Believe in the LORD your God, so shall ye be established; believe His prophets, so shall ye prosper."

My Biblical backing basis can be found in Second Chronicles. As we dissect the entire chapter that our spiritual 20/20 vision comes from, it becomes apparent that in the midst of your problems, prayer, prophecy, and praise will produce prosperity.

The twentieth chapter of Second Chronicles tells us a marvelous story. Jehoshaphat was the king of Judah, and he was warned that a great army had formed and was at that very moment moving against him. In actuality, several different nations had assembled and were on their way to completely destroy Judah.

I've learned that when your enemies are assembling against you, God will send you a word. We do not serve a God that—when you're in His divine will—will allow you to be ambushed by those plotting your demise. God will always send you a word if you are listening. God will always send warning before destruction. That's one of the reasons the book of Revelation says, "He that hath an ear, let him hear what the Spirit saith unto the churches." (Revelation 2:7, KJV)

THE PRAYER

So, upon hearing the warning, Jehoshaphat became afraid because in the natural he knew that he couldn't withstand the attack of this great army. So, the king did what any soldier growing up in the hood would do: he went looking for his backup. Jehoshaphat didn't have to look far because this great king knew that all his help cometh from the Lord. So, he set himself to see the Lord.

This initial example that Jehoshaphat displays is so important because, as I mentioned earlier, when we're faced with adversity, we get busy in the natural and invariably miss or hinder the spiritual move of God on our behalf. Remember that we as born-again believers need to set ourselves into a steadfast position where we can be still and seek God's face. Then, once we're in the right place, we've got to be sure that it's God we're hearing from. The reason being that the enemy knows that secret place also, and don't think he won't try to deceive you with two ounces of truth wrapped around twenty pounds of lies.

Once prayer has ushered us into the right place, sometimes we've also got to turn down our plates and fast. The Word of God, in the Gospel of Matthew, says "this kind goeth not out but by prayer and fasting." (Matthew 17:21, KJV) So, Jehoshaphat got the whole kingdom on one accord and fasted and prayed. He ensured that all flesh had been crucified, and the collective Spirit Man of the kingdom was strong.

The king ensured that nothing was coming between him and his Savior and that he could hear a word straight from God. To make it plainer, he extended his spiritual antennas to be certain that there was no static or interference. A great benefit of fasting is that it allows you to be more sensitive to any and everything around you.

So, Jehoshaphat assembled all Judah and Jerusalem together for a corporate prayer, and he got downright personal with God. When you know where you stand with God, then you can remind God where He stands with you. When you have a personal relationship with God, then as one of His children you remain in reverence, yet you can get intimately personal with your Daddy.

When you're in good standing with God, you can remind God of His promises. You can say with assurance, "God, You know that I'm a tither, and it was You that said all my needs would be met."

"God, I know I got this foreclosure notice, but it was You that gave me this house!"

"God, I know I got a repossession notice, but it was You that blessed me with this car!"

"God, I know that an undefeatable army is rising up against me, but it was You that promised me this land!"

THE PROPHECY

The Bible tells us that Jehoshaphat got the entire house in one accord and God's Glory saturated the courtyard. The Spirit of the LORD fell upon Jahaziel, and he prophesied such a mighty word that the great Gospel songstress Yolanda Adams is still singing it under the anointing today. Jahaziel said, "Don't worry about fighting that unbeatable army because this battle is not yours: it belongs to the LORD!" (Second Chronicles 20:15)

When you know who you are in Christ, our Heavenly Father will rarely let you lift a finger towards your enemies. Just recite the beginning of Psalm 35 and tell God to fight against them that are fighting against you! Pastor Dorothy Hughes taught me that God loves it when you give His word back to Him. Jahaziel continued by telling the kingdom to stand still and see the salvation of the Lord. "Be not dismayed. Just go out there tomorrow and position yourselves, for the Lord is with you." (Second Chronicles 20:17)

Phew! What a word, what a word, what a word!

And then Jahaziel offered unto the kingdom the spiritual 20/20 vision and he told them: "Believe in the LORD your God, so shall ye be established; believe his prophets, so shall ye prosper." (Second Chronicles 20:20, KJV)

THE PRAISE

The next five verses of the twentieth chapter of Second Chronicles are so powerful that we've got to just take a look and marvel at God's awesome wonder:

> [21] And when he had consulted with the people, he appointed singers unto the LORD, and that should praise the beauty of holiness, as they went out before the army, and to say, Praise the LORD; for his mercy endureth for ever.
>
> [22] And when they began to sing and to praise, the LORD set ambushments against the children of Ammon, Moab, and mount Seir, which were come against Judah; and they were smitten.
>
> [23] For the children of Ammon and Moab stood up against the inhabitants of mount Seir, utterly to slay and destroy them: and when they had made an end of the inhabitants of Seir, every one helped to destroy another.
>
> [24] And when Judah came toward the watch tower in the wilderness, they looked unto the multitude, and, behold, they were dead bodies fallen to the earth, and none escaped.
>
> **—2 Chronicles 2:21–24 (KJV)**

THE PROSPERITY

> [25] And when Jehoshaphat and his people came to take away the spoil of them, they found among them in abundance both riches with the dead bodies, and precious jewels, which they stripped off for themselves, more than they could carry away: and they were three days in gathering of the spoil, it was so much.
>
> **—2 Chronicles 2:25 (KJV)**

Oh, Hallelujah! Can you believe that? Can you even imagine that? The spoils were so abundant that it took THREE days to gather it!!! One for the Father, one for the Son, and one for the Holy Ghost! If you've never gotten excited about any prophetic word on prosperity, you'd better get excited about that.

Prayer, prophecy, and praise do produce prosperity! It's the wealth of the wicked, and it's been stored up just for us! If you are willing to consecrate yourself with prayer and fasting, then believe and receive.

Next, praise God like you've lost your mind, and you've already received the blessings that God has ordained you to have! There is no way that you can lose!

No devil in hell will be able to steal your inheritance. For we are a royal priesthood, a chosen generation, [1 Pet. 2:9] and when we give God all the glory and send perfected praises up, then He showers us with all His blessings raining down!

It happened then, and it's still happening now. Know and believe that in the midst of your problems, prayer, prophecy, and praise still produce prosperity.

CHAPTER 19:

PROSPERITY THROUGH SERVANTHOOD

Another way that God will prosper us is through servanthood. Truthfully speaking, ministry is all about serving God's people. The word *deacon* actually means 'servant'. Churches were established to serve as a place of worship as well as to serve the needs of the community.

Pastors were established to teach and preach God's Holy Word as well as to shepherd and serve the flock that God has entrusted to them. Accordingly, in God's protocol, the flock is to ensure that the men and women of God who are in authority over them are provided for and served with the respect that their positions demand.

As I'm writing this, Satan is in my ear saying that he thought it was God's responsibility to provide all our needs. You see, that's just like our adversary. The devil knows Scripture better than most believers and will often try and manipulate God's written Word to cause confusion in the church. However, God is not the author of confusion, and that's one of the reasons we are prompted to study, to show ourselves approved.

The fact of the matter is, YES, it is God who is the provider and supplier of all our needs. Yet First Timothy 5:17 (KJV) says, "Let the elders that rule well be counted worthy of double honour, especially they who labour in the word and doctrine."

Servanthood is a basic Biblical principle. We are commanded to serve the Lord our God with all our hearts. The Bible also gives us numerous examples of apprentices, armor-bearers, and disciples serving their personal lords and masters. I know that as a young man growing up in New Jersey in the 60's and 70's, when the Nation of Islam was flourishing there, the principle of Biblical servanthood was looked at as a means of keeping African-Americans in bondage. This fact, coupled with portrayals of a blond-haired, blue-eyed Jesus, led many people of color who were not spiritual away from Christianity.

The fact remains that Aaron served Moses. David served Saul. Jonathan served David. Joseph served Potiphar. Elisha served Elijah. The disciples served Jesus. And all those who served faithfully prospered in their due season. Only when you can see through spiritual eyes are you able to establish covenant relationships that postpone your own personal agenda to fulfill the vision of the one whom you are serving.

God loves and respects that protocol because He established it! You don't worship and serve your leaders as God, but you worship the God in your leader! Hello, somebody! And when you begin to acknowledge and reverence the God in your leader, then you have no issues with serving them. Then, when you begin to serve and bless the man or woman of God, the God of the man or woman will ultimately bless you for your faithfulness. You don't do it solely to get blessed, but your soul gets blessed from doing it!

In the books of First Kings and Second Kings, we learn of an example of such servanthood by studying two great prophets of God—Elijah and Elisha. God instructed Elijah to anoint Elisha to be a prophet. Elijah found the young man plowing with twelve yoke of oxen before him, and the Bible says that Elijah cast his mantle upon him.

Upon closer examination, you will find that Elisha did not mistake his prophetic summons. God didn't need to make him an offer that he couldn't refuse. Elisha didn't hesitate and his response was decisive. He symbolically burned his past behind him. He saw his profession as a farmer as merely external and immediately gave up his former life for his higher calling.

How many of us refuse to burn our past behind us and cling to that which is merely external and has no spiritual significance regarding what God has called us to be. Then we wonder why we struggle in our lives. It's because we haven't adhered to God's purpose for our lives, and therefore we cannot be in His Divine will.

But Elisha was different than most of us. This young man knew from the moment Elijah anointed him that he was called to be a servant to God's people. Before God could make him a chief servant helping many, Elisha understood that he had to be the humble servant to just one: Elijah.

Too many of us in ministry pray that God bless us with gifts of His Spirit, but we still don't want to serve. Make no mistake about it, God will not bless you to be served by anyone if you have never humbled yourself to serve someone else.

If you belong to a church, then God has given you a pastor after His own heart. That very man or woman of God is your Elijah. How are you serving your Elijah? Are you lifting up their arms the way that Aaron lifted Moses'? Are you serving your leader unconditionally with your whole heart the way that Elisha served Elijah?

Have you been more of a burden to them than a bearer, occupying their time with trivial and petty matters? Or are you serving them, but serving them conditionally? Will you serve them even if they openly rebuke you? Or once your little feelings get hurt, do you call yourself getting back at them by your refusal to continue in the blessed position that God has entrusted you with? If that is the case, then woe be unto you, for you will never prosper in that mindset.

I believe that our prosperity is contingent upon our servanthood. Let me say that again: *our prosperity is **contingent** upon our servanthood!* Hello, somebody! Webster's Dictionary defines *contingent* as 'dependent on or conditioned by something else'.

Third John 1:2 tells us that above all things God wishes that we may prosper. However, when a prophetic word is spoken into our lives from God, it is contingent upon our being in the will of God. God desires for us, who have been saved and sanctified, to perfect our ministries so that souls are won for His kingdom. Our ministries are vessels for our servanthood.

Look at the last sentence of verse First Kings 19:21 —

> And he returned back from him, and took a yoke of oxen, and slew them, and boiled their flesh with the instruments of the oxen, and gave unto the people, and they did eat. Then he arose, and went after Elijah, and ministered unto him.
>
> —1 Kings 19:21 (KJV)

He didn't preach to Elijah about his personal vision; instead, Elisha served Elijah. Ministry is servanthood.

I don't care if you disagree with me, but hopefully you've got enough sense to believe the Word of God. The Bible tells us that after Elisha had served Elijah faithfully, when Elijah knew that his end was near, he tried to get Elisha to tarry, or wait, while he went on.

Elisha would not dare leave this great man of God who had anointed him and become his closest friend. To Elijah's instructions that Elisha stay behind ("tarry") while he went ahead, Elisha responds twice in the same way:

> [4] And Elijah said unto him, Elisha, tarry here, I pray thee; for the LORD hath sent me to Jericho. And he said, As the LORD liveth, and as thy soul liveth, I will not leave thee. So they came to Jericho. [5] And the sons of the prophets that were at Jericho came to Elisha, and said unto him, Knowest thou that the LORD will take away thy master from thy head to day? And he answered, Yea, I know it; hold ye your peace. [6] And Elijah said unto him, Tarry, I pray thee, here; for the LORD hath sent me to Jordan. And he said, As the LORD liveth, and as thy soul liveth, I will not leave thee. And they two went on.
>
> —2 Kings 2:4–6 (KJV)

It was then, at the river Jordan, that Elijah used his mantle to divide the waters. When he and Elisha reached the other side, Elijah asked Elisha a question:

> And it came to pass, when they were gone over, that Elijah said unto Elisha, Ask what I shall do for thee, before I be taken away from thee. And Elisha said, I pray thee, let a double portion of thy spirit be upon me.
>
> —2 Kings 2:9 (KJV)

Once you have given yourself as a holy sacrifice unto the Lord and served faithfully with your whole heart, the Bible says that you may ask God what you will!

What does this have to do with prosperity? you may think. Well, prosperity is not only measured in material wealth, it is also and most importantly spiritual. When God prospers you in the spirit, that's when all your material needs are met. That's why Matthew 6:33 says "But seek ye first the kingdom of God, and his righteousness; and all these things shall be added unto you." (Matthew 6:33, KJV)

At our church, we received a prophetic word that the second half of the year was going to be better than the first half. Many of our members didn't embrace it because they failed to realize that it was in the spirit realm that we had been prospered. We must receive and believe our *spiritual* prosperity before the material prosperity will follow.

Before you can reap anything, you must first sow. This is true both in the natural and in the spiritual. I have come to believe that there are no coincidences in the Lord our God. So, make no mistake about it: Elisha, the former farmer, knew the principles of sowing and reaping, and he knew that *now* was his due season of harvest. So, he requested a double portion of Elijah's spirit so that he could live large and prosper, right? WRONG!

Elisha requested a double portion of Elijah's spirit so that he could be an even *greater* servant to the people of God! Hello, somebody! You see, when you have the heart of a servant, then you have the ear of God. When God knows that He can trust you with His anointing, then He knows that when His blessings begin to overtake you, you will have enough sense to pass the blessings on to others. The more you bless God's people, the more God will bless you.

Let me say that again: *The more you bless God's people, the more God will bless you.*

Now substitute the word "serve" for the word "bless": *The more you serve God's people, the more God will serve you.* You see, God's ways are not our ways, but once you begin to understand His ways, our way becomes prosperous! You receive by GIVING!

To receive life everlasting, you must first *give your life.*

To reap God's rewards, you must first sow into His kingdom.

To become a great leader, you must first *become a great servant*.

Elisha knew and understood God's principles, but make no mistake about it: Elisha did not serve Elijah so that he would become a great leader. However, by serving Elijah and God with his whole heart, God was commanded by His own word to make him great! In the Old Testament, Elijah is credited with having performed seven remarkable miracles. Elisha is credited with a whopping fourteen!

To me though, one of the things that made Elisha so awesome of a Godly example was the fact that he was known to have anointed kings, but he was also known to equally serve the common man with no respect of person.

Many of us pray for the great anointing of an Elisha, but too many of us want the *testimony* without going through the *test*. You may ask, "What do you mean, Brother Preacher?" What I mean is that there's a price to pay for the anointing. Allow me to reiterate: the anointing is costly! How badly do you want it? Many of us desperately desire to *prosper*, but we don't want to unconditionally *serve*.

"Not I," you may say. Well then, check this out: God has blessed many of us with the gift of spiritual discernment. And when we discern a holy man/woman of God in our midst, we should be compelled to care for them the way that Elisha cared for Elijah. How are you caring for *your* "Elijah"?

"Oh, I would care for them, but I was never given the title of Adjutant."

"Oh, I would care for them, but the last time I tried to help them, they snapped at me and hurt my feelings."

"Oh, I would care for them, but ain't no sense in me trying, 'cause the elders and ministers are always all around him and won't let you get close to him."

"Oh, I would care for him, but the Lord blessed me to get this second job for Christmas, and I got to get Pookie's gifts out of layaway and pay for this new Lexus God blessed me with."

"Oh, I would care for him, but I just gave him $100 last year."

Friends and saints of the Most High God, we will never prosper in God if we are not willing to humble ourselves and serve those who have been given authority over us. As I stated before, when we begin to take care of the man or woman of God, then the God of the man or woman will take care of us.

God's Word says that the wealth of the wicked is laid up for us, ^{Prov. 13:22} and also that He has given us power to get wealth, ^{Deut. 8:18} but until we are willing to serve, God will not prosper us.

In the fourth chapter of Second Kings, you will find the story of Elisha and the Shumanite woman. The Bible says that this woman was well-to-do, and that she noticed Elisha as he often traveled through her town. Through her true generosity, motivated by God's favor, she offered to feed Elisha as he passed.

So, Elisha would come and eat with her as he passed through her way. The woman noticed the mantle upon him and remarked to her husband that Elisha was a great man of God. She decided to prepare a room for Elisha on their roof, and so she furnished it and allowed him to retreat there as his travels dictated.

This woman knew that she was in the midst of a mighty man of God, so she was compelled to serve him. As a result of her servanthood, Elisha felt compelled to bless her. Elisha prophesied that in a year's time that she would be holding a son in her arms. He promised her this gift.

Being the great prophet that he was, in a year's time—just like he spoke it—the Shumanite woman held her son in her arms. A few years later, the Bible says that something happened to the boy. He ran to his father in the field saying that there was a problem with his head. At that, the father took the boy in to his mother who held the boy in her arms until he died shortly after. The woman then took the boy up into the prophet's room and laid him upon the prophet's bed.

I'm here to tell you that sometimes there is a test tied to your blessing. Sometimes God will bless us with something that we cherish and then challenge us to see if we are still worthy of that which He has blessed us with. This is true, because when we prove ourselves worthy of what we consider to be this great thing that in actuality turns out to be just a little thing to God, He rewardingly blesses us with something even greater, after we prove ourselves faithful.

"But why would God do such a thing?" you may ask. "Why would He bless us and then test us?" The reason is that often we cherish the gift but not the *gift giver*. Many times we serve the creation more than we do the Creator! ^{Rom. 1:25} Hello, somebody!

So, oftentimes we find that a test is associated with or tied to our blessing. Now, the true question is, how will we respond when this storm covers our path? How are we going to "carry it" through this predicament that we've found ourselves in?

Let's go back to the Bible and see what the Shumanite woman did. The Bible says that this woman, after laying the child upon the prophet's bed, sought out after the prophet. This tells me that you've got to go to the source of your blessing. You see, she could have complained to her husband or her girlfriends about this so-called man of God. She could have wrapped herself into a grief-stricken pity party. She could have murmured and complained, but not so, for she was a virtuous woman. ^{Prov. 31:10} So, she went back to the source.

So, now we must realize where our source lies. We no longer have to seek a priest or prophet to intercede on our behalf, but now, under our new and better covenant, we can go to God for ourselves. When you have developed a relationship with God, and the God of that relationship blesses you with something and then something happens to your blessing, you must seek God. Proverbs 10:22 (KJV) says, "The blessing of the LORD, it maketh rich, and He addeth no sorrow with it."

So, the Shumanite woman sought out the great man of God. When she found him and told him what had happened, Elisha came and lay upon the child. He prayed and lay upon the child again until the boy sneezed seven times and came back to life. Now, Elisha performed this miracle, but God got the glory!

To my knowledge, the Bible never mentions this family again, but if we could check the record, I'm sure we'd find that the seed of this woman, her fruit, was a blessing from God. I feel confident in saying that her seed grew strong and her fruit remains. You see, what good are blessings if they won't last?

John 15:16 (KJV) begins by saying, "Ye have not chosen me, but I have chosen you, and ordained you, that ye should go and bring forth fruit, and that your fruit should remain..."

The Bible says that our fruits are a living testimony to our relationship with and our servanthood to God. It is not only God's desire but it's also His intention for us to be fruitful. That's why He chose us. Not only did He choose us but He also ordained us to be fruitful and for our fruit to remain.

The Shumanite woman, although she was very well-to-do, esteemed Elisha higher than herself. We can't always wonder, what would Jesus do. Sometimes we need to just do like Jesus did! Borrow the slogan from Nike and say to yourself: JUST DO IT! Esteem another higher than yourself and be willing to wash another's feet. Uh-oh! Stop the press! I can hear some of you saying, "I ain't washing nobody's stinking feet."

Well, Jesus did it. I believe that act to be Jesus' greatest single example of true leadership. Jesus humbled Himself to wash the feet of His disciples. In fact, His disciple Peter said, "Lord, I cannot let You do this, for I am not worthy." And the Lord Jesus replied, "If you do not let Me do this, then you are not worthy!" [Jn. 13:8]

If you are willing to humble yourself to do this, then God will make you the head and not the tail. [Deut. 28:13] God will make you the lender and not the borrower. [Deut. 28:12] God will bless you coming in, and He will bless you going out. [Deut. 28:6]

God will give you an inheritance for your children's children. [Prov. 13:22] God will cause you to bear fruit, and your fruit will remain. [Jn. 15:16] You shall be like a tree planted by the rivers of water, whose leaf shall not wither, and whatsoever thou doest thou shall prosper. Ps. 1:3

But remember, your prosperity is contingent upon your servanthood. How are you serving your "Elijah"?

PART 5:

BENEDICTION

CHAPTER 20: TWENTY YEARS LATER

As the previous nineteen chapters chronicle, I was miraculously, instantaneously, and simultaneously delivered from drugs, alcohol, and tobacco in July of 1996. Today, nearly twenty-five years later, I find myself so far removed from that period in my life, that my addiction seems surreal—almost as if it happened to someone else.

Even though it's been a quarter-century, I now find myself fighting embarrassment that was non-existent when *From Crack to Christ* was initially released. Because of the new man God has desired I become, the life I lived then sometimes repulses me today. While I may be relatively surprised by my current reaction, obviously, God never is.

Accordingly, God reminds me in His word found in Matthew 6:27 (NRSV) "And can any of you by worrying add a single hour to your span of life?" In like manner, no one can change anything in our lives that has already transpired. So, why worry about it? God, in His infinite wisdom, deals with us not only according to where we are but also according to where He desires we be. Ergo, I find myself revisiting a conversation I had with the Lord when He told me to write this book. It went something like this:

God: I want you to write a book and tell your story of addiction.

Me: You want me to do what? *(long pause as I ponder excuses)* But, what about those people who will look at me differently?

God: Yes, there are those who will look at you differently. *(pause, giving me time to catch up)* But, I'm here to tell you that they weren't for you anyway. *(short pause)* And, besides, this isn't about you. This is about Me!

As they say, the rest is history. In this case, *HIS*tory! Looking back on my life, since that moment, God has never failed to do precisely what He said. Unfortunately, there are times when we can get sidetracked because the resemblance between what God promised and our circumstances is not a case of their being identical twins.

Since *From Crack to Christ* was first published, I have had two cars repossessed and experienced the foreclosure of our dream home. This traumatic foreclosure began when I was fired unfairly from my job. For the eight years leading up to my job dismissal, I worked as a consultant for a major tobacco manufacturer. I was blessed to almost double my salary as I vacated working for a hospital experiencing elevation as a Fortune 500 consultant.

My consulting opportunity manifested because I had experience working with both PC and Apple computers, and my skill set was needed to avert any IT infrastructure failures due to the Y2K threat. After Y2K turned out to be a dud, the company instituted a policy that consultants could only be employed by them for two consecutive years. Due to God's favor, I kept being retained and promoted in responsibility for eight successive years.

In my eighth year of consulting for this manufacturer, I then managed a team of engineers and developers responsible for 24-7 maintenance of their factory-floor automation. Previously, I worked at four different office campuses this leading manufacturer utilized. Finally, due to my new authority, I was relocated to the manufacturing center (the MC).

Several thousand employees worked there. Much of the upper management were a bunch of good ole' boys! The majority of black women hired were eye-candy (albeit also qualified). Profanity was the language of choice, and the staff were allowed to smoke cigarettes everywhere in the building except on the highly flammable factory floor.

After only two weeks at the MC, I conceded that this was undoubtedly the most ungodly place I ever worked! I recall asking God, "Why in the world would you send me here?" Then I found out about an employee-run Christian group meeting weekly called "Hands Up!". This group, for me, was a slice of heaven!

God's response to my question was Matthew 16:18 (KJV) "And I say also unto thee, That thou art Peter, and upon this rock I will build my church; and the gates of hell shall not prevail against it."

Hands Up not only provided a place for strengthening believers by allowing "iron to sharpen iron", Prov. 27:17 but we also did community outreach over the holidays! We financially blessed several families as well as gave away dozens of bicycles to the inner-city housing complexes. The group leaders often supported each other in our ministry efforts outside of work. The most significant benefit for me was that the Lord blessed me with a lifelong friend and sister for life in Ruth Johnson.

Let's rewind, back to my firing. There was an incident where a cordial racist, who worked for the manufacturer, used the "N-word" in a conversation with me. Since it wasn't directed at me, I took it in stride. Then, a few weeks later, he verbally attacked me because of something his director instructed me to do. This time it was a heated exchange. I immediately told his (white female) director that this was the last time I would stand for any disrespect from this racist individual.

At the time, I was unaware that because I stood up, this racist's director called my consulting firm and told them that they no longer wanted me to work at their company. However, I'd just received a glowing annual performance review from my director; therefore, firing me would've been litigation-risky. My consulting firm then put a plan in place to have me removed.

First, they reassigned my director, with whom I shared a great relationship. They placed me under the authority of the director who managed our account. He and I had a one-on-one meeting, and he asked if I would be interested in filling a new role they were creating. This role, he explained, was more suited to my strengths, which were the relationships I had made in the previous eight years at the manufacturer. With this promotion, I would function as an account liaison overlooking our operations.

I took the bait, hook, line, and sinker. In the next few weeks, I trained my replacement. Then, when it was time to transition into my new role, I was told that the funding for my position was voted down, and the new role was placed on hold. As a result, I received a small severance package, and let go. Several months later, the director who managed that account admitted to me over the phone that he had lied! He nonchalantly confessed that the whole thing had been a hoax to get rid of me because the client suddenly wanted me gone. He never apologized, though!

I was incensed! I was so furious that if I were in the presence of this man, I would have seriously hurt him for having the arrogance to tell me that he lied to me! They had no regard for putting my family's livelihood in jeopardy! This man was ten years younger than me, yet he had had several open-heart surgeries! I had to repent to God because all I could think about was how enjoyable it would be to stomp a mudhole in his chest!

What followed were six months of hell! I found myself emotionally drained after fighting with the lenders of several predatory housing loans! As that market crashed, as I watched my mortgage payments double, as I continually fought over the phone with bill collectors threatening foreclosure, I made the painful decision to abandon our home.

My wife was devastated! I felt as though I had let my family down! How could this happen to obedient children of God? I had never stopped serving in ministry. I previously served as a deacon and was recently elevated to a minister! I was a tither! I was faithful to the church and its people! *How could this happen?*

I was so hurt that, after twenty years of living in Chesterfield County, Virginia, I was through with them! I swiftly and wholly relocated my family across the river, thirty miles north in Glen Allen! Through my hurt emotions, embarrassment, and feelings of failure, the Lord still kept me and never ceased to encourage me.

The Spirit of the Lord showed me of all the good things that transpired even during that chaos! In retrospect, I was the only black manager working for that consulting firm. There were three white managers, one manager from India, and me. It was a blessing that while there, the firm paid for my training as a certified project manager. As a result, I earned my PMP credentials! Then, one of the directors of the tobacco manufacturer who befriended me retired and began consulting himself. He started working for a trucking company and insisted that they hire me as a project manager at that company!

Additionally, during that season, I'd gone to the local seminary to inquire about a formal preaching course. I met with a Rev. Debra Martin who saw something in me. She asked if I would consider enrolling in Seminary in a master's program. I was somewhat perplexed because I didn't have a bachelor's degree. So, I had to take some tests, write a paper, and then my admission had to be approved by the dean. While under consideration amid this process, I was allowed to attend the orientation where Dean Kinney preached at the luncheon a sermon entitled, "Going to the Other Side!"

I found myself captivated! Dean Kinney absolutely blew my mind! There was no doubt that he was the most skilled orator I ever heard! I was also convinced that the Samuel DeWitt Proctor School of Theology at Virginia Union University was where I belonged! The Lord favored me, and I was accepted into their Master of Divinity curriculum, even though I didn't have a bachelor's degree!

Look at God, the Master Encourager! Smack dab in the middle of my persecution—God's promotion sought me out.

Through my years of addiction, I'd forgotten just how much I loved to learn! Still healing from the trauma of losing our home, working full-time, and serving in ministry, I attended classes two nights a week and on weekends! This schedule would be my routine for the next four years! Their seminary process broke you down by forcing you to unlearn your previous conceptions of religion and God. Then the process strengthened your foundation, rebuilding you as a broader-thinking, more inclusive, ethics-based, community theologian.

Many of my classmates dropped out at various stages of this stress-filled, three-year process. Yet, the Lord my God sustained me through the seminary experience, as well as the real-life drama—or "light affliction" 2 Cor. 4:17 — that temporarily defined me. Determined to "trust the process", I found myself immersed in Second Corinthians 4:16-18.

> [16] For which cause we faint not; but though our outward man perish, yet the inward man is renewed day by day. [17] For our light affliction, which is but for a moment, worketh for us a far more exceeding and eternal weight of glory; [18] While we look not at the things which are seen, but at the things which are not seen: for the things which are seen are temporal; but the things which are not seen are eternal.
>
> **—2 Corinthians 4:16-18 (KJV)**

After being out of college for over fifteen years, even though I never completed my bachelor's degree, I earned my Master of Divinity degree, finishing 12th in my class of over 250 graduates.

This accomplishment was a tremendous confidence builder, not so much in my ability, but primarily regarding the excellent work God wants to complete in me!

> Being confident of this very thing, that he which hath begun a good work in you will perform it until the day of Jesus Christ
>
> **—Philippians 1:6 (KJV)**

Unsure of the next steps in my educational journey, I stayed put at Samuel DeWitt Proctor School of Theology at Virginia Union University and studied an additional year, earning a second master's degree—a Master of Arts in Christian Education. This time I amassed a 3.98 GPA, tying for the highest GPA in that graduating year.

No one can doubt that the favor of God rests upon my life. The seminary experience is a divine calling requiring God's grace and mercy to navigate it successfully.

My friend, the late Bishop David Wallace (who in the year 2000 tarried with me until I received the baptism of the Holy Ghost) once stated, "If God gives you an assignment, and the enemy doesn't come against you, I doubt very seriously that your assignment came from God."

In the coming months, that knowledgeable warning again amplified in the form of my employment. I found myself fired from a second job for no good reason! On this occasion, I was consulting as a senior IT project manager/business analyst for the IT department of the transportation company mentioned earlier. The owners of the privately-owned company decided to bring in a new CEO of IT. Over half of the IT staff were let go and replaced with the new CEO's appointments in the next few months.

Again, since I had strong relationships and stellar performance, it was problematic to simply oust me. This time, I found myself accused of sending a contentious email fostering dissension by attacking a developer's findings—hardly an offense worthy of firing, if true; certainly a travesty if untrue. The recipient of the obviously "cut-and-paste" email (supposedly from me) was conveniently "out of town". My friend from the tobacco industry was conveniently "on vacation". Our IT wizards searched my laptop for hours but found no existence of the email I supposedly sent. Really? That's the best you can do, devil? Nevertheless, they first sent me home; the next day they asked me not to return.

The ugly scenario of my family's lack of housing security unfortunately repeated. Being out of work for five months, I was taken to court and evicted from the beautiful four-thousand square foot, executive-style home we'd been renting for the previous three years. The judge gave us ten days to move.

For a period of nearly a month in 2012 we were homeless. However, we were never hopeless! After loading our things into storage, my wife, two daughters and I moved into a one-room, extended-stay hotel. Remarkably, by the grace of God, my family grew closer together and were strengthened during this season of transition.

Despite the lies to me and the lies told about me, I was living out Genesis 50:20.

> You intended to harm me, but God intended it for good to accomplish what is now being done, the saving of many lives.
>
> —**Genesis 50:20 (NIV)**

Our hotel was located in Glen Allen, just outside of the Innsbrook IT and Business community. Our room was on the second floor, on the back corner of the complex. There was a road that ran alongside our room, separating us from a strip mall. Yet, I often wondered where that road, alongside our room, led. It seemed to be an office campus of some kind, but I never journeyed that way.

Fast forward eighteen months. At that time, I was employed as a senior IT project manager for the healthcare company where I currently work. I was facilitating a meeting in the fifth and top floor conference room of our building. I had consultants on the line from India and other programmers, analysts, and developers present—all under my authority. While standing at the head of the conference table, I happened to glance out the window, and I saw it!

It was the corner hotel room we stayed in when we were homeless! This building where I was now gainfully employed was at the end of that road that I previously wondered about! For a few seconds, I was speechless, struggling to regain my composure! After the meeting, I stared out the window at this view, fighting back the tears. The Lord had literally lifted me above my situation and my circumstances! My colleagues and co-workers, who highly respected me, had no idea that 18 months earlier, my family and I were homeless living a stone's throw away from my current place of employment!

Four months after settling into our new home—two days after Christmas, December 27th, 2012—my urologist informed me that I was diagnosed with prostate cancer. While I vividly recall that consultation, I have no recollection of what the physician said after stating those three words no one wants to hear: "You have cancer."

Even more challenging was having to see the look on my family's faces after telling them. My wife, daughters, and mother all fought back their tears. Our Christmas celebration unintentionally became something else. In the midst, I recalled something that severely struck me in Chapter One, and that is the peace of God!

The peace of God that passes all understanding allowed me to hold it together for my family! That peace and a prevailing sense of calm empowered me to learn as much as possible about my variation of this dreaded disease. The more I learned, the more God assured me I'd be alright.

So, when some doctors told me to rush and have my prostate removed, I said, I'm not doing it. When other doctors suggested I have the laser treatment, my response was God isn't telling me that! Unless God tells me something specific to do, then I will stand still and see His salvation! And now, nearly eight years later, my PSA numbers have only increased a few one-hundredths of a point. I stepped out on my faith, and once again, the Lord our God continues to show Himself strong!

Twenty years later, my story may help those associated with me understand why I don't have time for so-called Christian leaders backstabbing and plotting the demise of other Christian leaders. They can miss me with all that! Hopefully, you'll know why Church foolishness and activities counter-productive to the upbuilding of God's Kingdom are for someone else. I've been through too much. I've come too far! This lifestyle is not a game for me! I'm not NEW to this, but I am TRUE to this! I must be about my Father's business! ^{Lk. 2:49}

Accordingly, please allow me to reassure someone else that you are stronger than you may know or realize—just as some go to a gym to get stronger and build muscle. In a sense, *From Crack to Christ: Twenty Years Later* is a spiritual workout allowing you also to develop your spiritual muscle and strengthen your faith.

In this season, because of everything I've faced, endured, and overcome... I'm still standing! No, I'm more than just standing.

> I press toward the mark for the prize of the high calling of God in Christ Jesus.

> **—Philippians 3:14 (KJV)**

Luke 12:48 tells us that to whom much is given, much is also required! Because of everything God has given me, it is not only a requirement, but it is also my pleasure to help and serve others! That is why I tell my story in such a transparent manner. In His infinite wisdom, our magnificent God knew this would happen when He called me to go from crack to Christ!

God bless you. My prayer is that this book has blessed, strengthened, encouraged, and inspired you to tell someone else of the Gospel or good news of our Lord and Savior, Jesus Christ.

It was He who delivered me from years of drug abuse and multiple life-threatening addictions.

It was He who showed me the glorious light illuminating His path of righteousness.

It was He that gave me the peace that surpasses all earthly understanding. Php. 4:7

It was He that strengthened me with His joy that truly is unspeakable. 1 Pet. 1:8

It was He that kept my mind while others around me were losing theirs.

It was He that first loved me before I ever could love myself.

It was He that cleansed, saved, and forgave me when it appeared that I was headed for destruction.

And it was He that brought me to this place where I could finally embrace my destiny and go from crack to Christ.

May God keep you in health and safety and abundantly bless and continually prosper you.

ACKNOWLEDGMENTS

Above all else, I give thanks to God, my Heavenly Father, for first saving a wretch like me, for sanctifying me, and filling me with the precious gift of His Holy Ghost. Father, your never-ending grace, mercy, unmerited favor, and abundant blessings never cease to amaze me. Just when I think that I know Your ways, You absolutely astound me with something that's completely beyond my wildest imagination. God, I owe everything to You, for without You there can be no me.

Even now, twenty years later, I still fight back tears grasping everything You've masterfully brought me through. Thank You for allowing me not to be overtaken by the devourer. Finally, Father, I thank You because You're doing exactly what You said.

To my beautiful, powerfully anointed, and loving wife, Lady Kimberly Towns: from day one, you have always been so precious to me. You have truly endured and now, your due season of exaltation has begun. Thank you for continuously living holy before me. Thank you for always covering me in prayer. Thank you for being my partner in ministry and life!

To my children and now grands—Steve Jr., Kelli, Tramia, Jace and Lotus: I am so grateful to be your Dad and your Papa. You all mean the world to me!

To my mother, father, and Mama Joyce: I love you all immensely! My prayer is that you want for nothing in this season of your lives.

To My Real Life Ministries family: You have all loved me uncon-ditionally! Our best is truly yet to come!

To my Grace Fifth family—Bishop Dwight L. Green, Sr., Bishop Chad Carlton, Supt. Clarence Sellers, Jr., and all of the Pastors and First Ladies, the Roanoke District, and our great Jurisdiction: You have no idea how much your leadership, brotherhood, mentorship, fellowship, and friendship have meant! We are forever connected!

To Dr. Wade Runge: Time and time again, you have proven that you are my big brother from another mother! "Thank you" doesn't seem adequate. How can I ever repay you? Know that I will do my best to ensure that this shepherd always smells like his sheep!

To Evangelist Shelly Miles and Fresh Fire Evangelistic Ministries, Bishop Phillip Green, Pastor Clemson Leech, Bishop Charles Connor, Bishop Elijah Hankerson, Dr. Dorinda Clark-Cole, Bishop Linwood Dillard, Supt. Waverly Bumbry, Supt. William Ward, Chairman Michael Eaddy, and Chairman Michael Golden, Jr.: Thank you all for opportunities to serve!

To my Regent University family—Dr. Patterson, Dr. Bekker, Dr. Doublestein and Dr. Silverstone, and our 2018-2019 cohort: Thank you all for stretching me in such a God-pleasing and powerful way!

ABOUT THE AUTHOR

A servant leader and gifted facilitator, Superintendent Dr. Stephen Brian Towns, Sr. is the Pastor and Founder of Real Life Ministries, Church of God In Christ. Having survived 28 years of substance abuse, then experiencing miraculous delivery simultaneously from drugs, alcohol, and tobacco, he is uniquely equipped to break down, dissect, and translate addiction and recovery from a spiritual perspective. He has served in ministry for over twenty years, touching countless lives internationally. His transformational storytelling resonates with his listeners, whether imprisoned behind bars or leaders behind boardroom tables.

From 2009–2013, Dr. Towns earned a Master of Divinity and a Master of Arts in Christian Education from the esteemed Samuel DeWitt Proctor School of Theology at Virginia Union University. Dr. Towns graduated from Regent University's Doctor of Strategic Leadership (DSL) program in May 2019 with a concentration in Healthcare Leadership after completing his doctoral coursework and a groundbreaking final project (The Importance of Psychological Safety in Today's Multicultural Healthcare Environment). Accordingly, Towns serves as the Director of Community Health and Human Services for his Jurisdiction.

On the National level for the Church of God in Christ, Dr. Towns serves as a consultant for the National Pastors and Elders Council Health Commission, and as the Director of the

International Department of Evangelism eNewsletter, The Evangelist Speaks, since its inception in 2012.

Pastor Towns' global ministry began when, in 2016, he visited Soweto, Johannesburg, Cape Town, and Durbin, South Africa. While there, he was blessed to preach in Pretoria and Johannesburg. Accordingly, with a heart for Nelson Mandela's homeland, in 2018 he was honored by being named Regional Evangelism President of South Africa by Bishop Charles Connor. He was also blessed with the Holy experience of being baptized in Israel's Jordan River in December of 2013.

Pastor Towns is committed to being a lifelong learner who loves to teach. He takes pride in being a voice for the voiceless and a defender of those unable to defend themselves. Bi-vocational, Dr. Towns currently serves in a senior role for a major healthcare organization. By leading ministries and the healthcare industry with principles of psychological safety, he endeavors to ensure that diversity, inclusion, and equity become the norm for marginalized peoples' collective advancement.

Dr. Towns resides in Henrico, Virginia where he is heavily involved in community service. In August of 2020, his ministry gave away over 144,000 pounds of food for COVID relief. An avid sports enthusiast, Dr. Towns is well-known as a local referee officiating basketball for over twenty-two years, excelling in high school, college, and on the semi-pro levels. In his leisure time, Dr. Towns and Kimberly, his wife of 32 years, enjoy traveling and cruising. He also adores spending time with his two grandchildren, Jace and Lotus.

Further information and resources about Pastor Towns and his ministry can be found on his website: www.StephenBTowns.com